DARK HORSES

and

BLACK BEAUTIES

Animals, Women, a Passion

Melissa Holbrook Pierson

Granta Books
London

Granta Publications, 2/3 Hanover Yard, London N1 8BE

First published in the United States by
W. W. Norton & Company, Inc., 2000
First published in Great Britain by Granta Books 2001

A CIP catalogue record for this book
is available from the British Library.

3 5 7 9 10 8 6 4 2

ISBN 1 86207 422 4

Printed and bound in Great Britain
by Mackays of Chatham plc

A Robin Red breast in a Cage
Puts all Heaven in a Rage
A dove house filld with doves & Pigeons
Shudders Hell thro all its regions
A dog starvd at his Masters Gate
Predicts the ruin of the State
A Horse misusd upon the Road
Calls to Heaven for Human blood

—WILLIAM BLAKE,
from "Auguries of Innocence"

These horses . . . these children, this toil and fun of
it all. The chat about "straight shoulders" and the gossip about "square quarters," the small profit and
extreme loss account at the gymkhanas, the grappling
with the horses, divorced from the ritual of grooms
which is our luck and joy. All this is yours and mine
and most people don't taste it in the same way. . . . How
right I am to write a book about "girls and horses."

—ENID BAGNOLD,
letter, 1934

CONTENTS

1

TIME MACHINE

I WOULDN'T MIND feeling it again, the first time I fell in love. Everyone has her own story, and everyone loses it somewhere down the line in the bottom of a drawer along with several broken keychains. Hard to believe that it once was the pulsating center of the known universe, your love, and the energy flew off it like those eruptions on the surface of the sun, spurting thousands of miles into space. But that was so long ago.

There remain buried bits of concrete evidence that I lived such a life, and with a little amateur archaeology, I can find what is left after the rains of time have expunged the mass of it. This year, as I stand on the edge of middle age, my mother dismays me by continuing to clean away my history. She has wallpapered my old room, the one I have not lived in for any length of time since 1976, and therefore removed the hanging shelves with glass-fronted vitrine she had bought for me when my model horse collection had outgrown all other furniture. When I saw the denuded state of my room on a recent visit, I involuntarily yelled, "Where are my horses?" and then ran down to the basement to ascertain that they were indeed safe in paper bags. But they nonetheless struck me as sad to be there now.

There are also some ribbons in a drawer, from the kind of childhood show in which everyone receives a ribbon; since a couple of these are blue rather than white or yellow, they lead me to believe they were won by my little sister.

Another room, in the basement, calls for more imaginative reconstructive history, since at first look nothing indicates its past importance as the headquarters for the Horse Club. There were only two members, the archival material reminds us, and the duration of its active life was relatively short, since one of the two broke the unspoken rules by actually *getting a horse*. Thus she had no more time to spend in the company of her friend in the friend's basement, putting up educational exhibits and keeping the scrapbook up to date. And even if she did, she would no doubt have wanted to avoid her friend's hurt looks and jealous pokings. So there, all that remains, if you scan the room closely, are some faded Magic Markered words above empty nails: HOOF PICK; ALUMINUM RACESHOE.

This is what is left of it all. Of the desire and the drive, of the longing and the dreaming, the months and years in thrall to an animal.

IT IS NOT my way to be simplistically reductive, but if someone threatened a day in the stocks over it, I would be forced to say that Carl Jung can be boiled down to one thing: balderdash. In part that is because he did not address the one archetype that runs through the culture like a root waiting to burst from the soil everywhere to grow thousands of genetically identical plants, amazing the populace as if each time it recurs it were some kind of miracle. Then again, maybe it is a miracle.

MARGARET CABELL SELF, the author of more than a dozen books, anthologies, and an encyclopedia of horses and horseman-ship, is precise in dating the beginning of the "love" era of the horse (as opposed to the pragmatic one, which has lasted for mil-lennia): March 1942. This happens to be when the United States cavalry was disbanded, and around the time when civilians became eligible to ride on the international jumping teams. "At the same time a curious thing occurred. Almost simultaneously and practi-cally throughout the country, children of all ages suddenly discov-ered the romance and fascination of the horse."

It might be added that boys were already well acquainted with it through the agency of war, which coated all instruments there-of with romance and fascination. It was girls who were now suddenly permitted to scramble over the ruins of the abandoned battlefield.

A simultaneous deconsecration of the horse, from the church of the economy, was necessary before the animal—with the exception of those involved in still viable industries such as rac-ing—was finally left to women. The last census of farm horses in this country was undertaken by the Department of Agriculture in 1959; it counted 3,089,000. The high point of the United States horse population was in 1918, when there were 21,550,000 work-ing in cities and on farms.

In *Horses of Today* (1964), Self goes on to explain what hap-pened to the first generation of these children under the influence of equine romance:

> They found that learning to become a good or even a passable rider was a long, tedious, often uncomfortable, and sometimes rather terrifying process. The boys espe-cially, who had less patience than the girls and to whom

the schools offered diversion in the form of organized sports, often lost interest. But for the girls riding was an ideal sport. They were quite contented to trot around and around while they were learning to talk "horse language." The psychological boost was enormous, not only finding themselves atop a horse but also discovering that, with patience, they could learn to control an animal far larger and stronger than themselves. Furthermore, here was a sport in which, as a sex, they were not handicapped in competition. Indeed they often showed greater sensitivity which made them excel over the boys, especially in the show ring.

FINDING SOMEONE TO talk to. Do you know what a desperate, aching quest this can be? We are pack animals, like our friends the dogs, and the feeling of being alone is etched into our DNA as a warning of the highest urgency: Do not stay here. We scramble and scratch the paint off the door, whining as if our hearts were breaking, which they are.

I have recently bought an old farm with a bit of land. I walk through the abandoned pastures and into the woods, where I see things that suddenly bring other things back. I used to know what this tree is; I used to know to suck on the stems of sassafras leaves and when the trilliums bloomed. I knew what things were called. I have the sensation of running through woods, though not these woods.

In the large maple tree in the center of my parents' brick terrace one branch stood out as a superior perch for a writer. My pencils and erasers would swing in a basket tied to it by string; my mother would call in a worried voice for me to climb down or I was going to fall and kill myself. I would stay up there and write stories about boys (the best protagonists, since they could do anything) who ran away to live in the woods with their faithful dogs. Away from their mothers. And away from the feeling of being alone in a world full of people.

There was someplace better, and there was someone who

understood, even though it was an animal who did not speak our language but rather a superior, deeper one.

And then the image of a horse struck my eyes. In it was something that vibrated below the level of hearing, below that of thought. Here was something that could bear me away, and all the outcasts who could find no one to talk to.

So it is first the way they look, both to and at us, that pins us flat. It is a magisterial beauty, no doubt about it. We don't know what to call it—art, genius—but we simply think, That is the most gorgeous thing I've ever seen. You fall in love with them entire, from a bit of a distance, not unlike the first time you really saw a boy: details cohering into one seductive picture, including knobby knees, the way the white socks drooped alluringly, the squinty eyes beneath blond lashes. The constituent parts of the horse, if not the boy, are joined in irreducibly perfect balance (and if I seem to project my aesthetic theories onto them, go ahead and snort, but horses are no less gorgeous post-snort, you'll see).

They are a stirringly impossible mixture of power and delicacy, size and fragility. They inspire fear even as they are filled with it themselves. They are wild and they are utterly tamable. All of this paradox is telegraphed by their bodies: an ankle you can fit your hand around and slender legs supporting the great barrel and muscled rump; the fluttering of sensitive ears and nostrils; the artistic curve of neck and the drapery of Pre-Raphaelite mane; the quickness, the dance; the eyes, oh the eyes—one of the largest in the animal kingdom, the great pools of assessment and expression that people frequently feel are the most beautiful thing about a horse. They are framed with lovely lashes. Even the males are pretty, as the females are powerful, and so horses seem to bear the same secret a little girl does about her own protean qualities even if the whole world would deny them. The relative size of these eyes, to get scientific about it, appeals at a primitive level to our instinct to nurture, since infants of many species draw us in with eyes that are large for their faces (see also kitsch of the collectible doll and puppy on china plate sort).

Best, the eyes call silently. They observe when we want nothing more than to be seen.

So now we are gripped by the desire to get nearer, and it is a desire that is more like a need. Up close we will find more: the large veins roaming over the fine bones of the face, the muzzle like velvet, the transporting scent of sweetness blown through the nostrils. We suck it up, the heady perfume. We run our hands over the body and its warm hair that sticks to our fingers. And we talk to the horse, who seems to listen. At least he doesn't say no.

THE BARN MEANS, first of all, a sweet smell—the hay, the molasses feed, the manure, the thousand breaths expelled by its denizens, breaths from a dark, moist interior that must be, she imagines, home somehow to wildflowers. There is dirt. Although everyone on the outside is always yammering about dirt—oh, no, not that!—no one mentions it here. One girl goes through the entire day with a green-brown smudge across her cheek that disappears into the corner of her mouth. Bits of hay fleck clothing; clots of manure stick to boots. There is ample chance for injury, scratches and bruises and rope-burn and certainly blisters. Muscles strain: move that pitchfork fast, throw that bale, run that wheelbarrow up the pile, scrub that tack till it shines. The giant ouch when a horse lands his hoof square on your foot. The tailbone thump, or the elbow crack, when you take your hundredth tumble into the sand. The sweat that pours as you are told to go around once more at a posting trot without stirrups.

Little girls are fragile things. They love their dolls and their dress-up. They are not naturally aggressive. They are afraid of spiders and dead mice.

They keep their secrets well when they leave the barn.

2

SYMPTOMOLOGY

THE MOTHERS PONDER: Where did this come from? They did not feed it next to the applesauce at lunch, or wrap it up as a birthday present. They did not sing about it at bedtime or read out loud about it from a book. They did not, to their knowledge, mention the name. But suddenly, nothing exists but horse. Their daughters have gone crazy; they are acting downright besotted.

Nothing less than the entire self undergoes transformation. They have, to themselves, become horses. Two legs instead of four is a mere speck of dust on the surface of the endeavor; see, forelegs alone in a syncopated beat yields a canter that could continue rocking for miles. The girls discover at last why their hair is long. A toss of the head, and there is mane along your neck. *Time* magazine in 1950 put the case down to the effect of Hopalong Cassidy: "even to the horselike galloping which had become as *de rigueur* among seven-year-old girls (who also whinnied occasionally) as the slouch among debutantes of the '20s." But this is no fad and could never have come from something as filmily distant as the movies. Instead it arises from the deep well of fluids that animate life itself. ("The Hullocks were blackening as Velvet cantered down the chalk road to the village. She ran on her own slender legs, making horse-noises and chirrups and occasionally striking her thigh with a switch, holding at the same time something very small before her as she ran.")

To others, they have become simply cute. One girl earnestly explains to her parents that when she runs, she is a horse; when she runs with a ribbon in her hair, she is a *wild* horse. To her it is not cute. It is the first time she has lived.

WHEN CONSTRAINED, CORRALLED, unable to transsubstantiate for the moment, as in the classroom, another vehicle is required. The pencil endlessly dances along the margin, creating herd after herd. Some specialize in heads, forelock this way then that. The more ambitious create whole standing forms, even if the hocks do not exactly adhere to nature. At this very moment, thousands and thousands of little girls are poised over their paper, wondering if the pastern should slope quite so much. It is as if their eye is offended to look on anything that does not contain the beguiling form of a horse.

HOW QUICKLY THEY become consummate autodidacts! Evolution, history, biology—nothing is too deep or too wide for their minds, so long as it has to do with . . . Before they know what their own bodies have been made for, they know the mechanisms of breeding, and they have looked at any number of pictures show-

ing a stallion covering a mare, or the foal halfway out and still covered by the gray skin of the amniotic sac. (This is part of their
secret education in the true ways of the world, which progresses
largely unbeknownst to parents and pals. It is their introduction to
the muck and dirt and grunts and blood that are, in the end, the
true story of everything.)

They may not read their *Weekly Reader,* but they have read
four-hundred-page equine encyclopedias. They can tell you that
some breeds of draft horse go back to the age of the conquerors
and the need for heavy stock to withstand a knight in full armor,
just as they know that the changing face of warfare soon favored
the light and swift instead. They've studied the evolutionary charts
and the breed charts and the color charts. You might have saved
yourself a pile of money had you known the only volume of the
family *Encyclopaedia Britannica* they would ever voluntarily look in
is the one labeled *H.*

Paper takes on importance, many, many bits of paper, fostering
nascent archival tendencies. On a trip to a feed store (they have no
horse—*yet,* they always add to themselves—but have found a way to
visit a feed store) they collect every Purina brochure and order form
for more information, on anything, including electric fencing and
modular barns. The postman daily brings the wish books filled with
stuff in which to dress a horsey dream—the Dover catalog, the
Stateline Tack and Valley Vet and Riding Right catalogs, and copies of
Horse & Rider, Equus, Horse Illustrated, Western Horseman, Young Rider.
Postcards, newspaper clippings, instruction sheets. The first scrapbook has long been filled, and the second and third are under way.

There is so much impulse behind the educational drive that
even the driest veterinary tract becomes delectable. They are
expanding and expanding. No matter how much more is out
there—and on the subject of the horse, it is unbelievable how
much more is out there—they are eager to consume it too.

EVER MORE SHELF SPACE is required. Existing volume within a room in which the eye does not encounter representations of

the favored animal is wasted space. Hence the race to fill it with models—any will do, plastic, papier-mâché, porcelain; but the ne plus ultra of the inanimate miniature is the Breyer horse. Once the province solely of little girls, and these days sculpted for the company exclusively by women, now the attention to detail lavished on this molded plastic model has paid off in large sales to adults, who personalize them and take them to shows where the competition is hardly less fierce than in a real ring. You can buy as many accoutrements as you can for a real horse—buckets, blankets, dandy brushes and mane combs, tack, hay bales, jumps, halters— but if you want manure, you make it yourself (the recipe for dung to scale: raw kernels of popcorn painted glossy olive, stuck together in clumps of three or four). Manes and tails may be brought to within inches of life by gluing on real hair strand by strand. At the shows, the judges often have experience as real show judges, so they would know, for instance, that in the barrel-racing "event," your horse should not have been posed at that particular angle at that particular spot. These are horses for people who can't have horses.

DREAMING, URGENT DREAMING. Sometimes it takes place during the day, but the dreamer is no less somnambulant for that. If a mother can't reach her daughter, it is because even though she stands in the kitchen, she is gathering her courage to walk up the driveway to that strange house she always stares at on the way to piano lessons, the only one left in the area with more than a spit of land—and behold, two well-aged nags in the barbed-wired backyard. She is going to knock on the door, and the old lady who answers will soon ask her in, give her some stale lemon cookies, and divulge the fact that she has been feeling lonely for young company, and, come to think of it, so have her horses. Would you like to have one of them? she will ask.

During the night your own house is transformed. One time it seems so clear, so powerfully true—the toolshed is now home to a pony, standing in deep straw, looking out the window, waiting for you to come and let it out into the side yard, now fenced with split rails even though the house lot is all told only one-half acre in a dense neighborhood of hundreds of other half-acre lots—that when you wake in the morning and rush outside to see that the toolshed is still filled only with shovels, sleds, and the lawn mower, you sink to the grass and weep.

3

REASON FOR BEING

THE WHOLE THING: a fluke of conformation. If the horse did not have a back this long and that pleasantly curved, and legs exactly this strong, we would have lost more than five thousand years of literature, numerous myths, much art, and an entire culture with its own language and customs. And untold else. Sophocles, even way back then, declared the taming of "the wild horse windy-maned" one of humanity's greatest accomplishments. Given time, we can calculate what we got out of it.

Unlike the descendants of wolves, who partnered with humans in a mutually beneficial arrangement, horses were handed the short straw before anyone even asked them if they wanted to play the game. Under domestication, they got mostly death by the billions in war, work, and as sacrifices to various gods, in exchange for a bit of grain and hay when all the while the preferable grass was free. If they weren't so well suited to the needs of man, their species would have been eradicated by hunting many thousands of years ago, which would have meant mainly many thousands of years of misery they would not have had to endure. (If it sounds unlikely for Paleolithic man, with his rough tools and small numbers, to do in a swift and widespread animal, consider the fact that bones from *tens of thousands* of horses were stacked in front of the cave of Solutré, near Lyons, which was inhabited by only a handful of families.) "Thou shalt be favored above all other creatures, for to thee shall accrue the love of the master of the earth," says the Koran in cursing the horse. Today a wealthy woman explains to a child why her Dutch warmblood must stay in his stall instead of going out at night to graze with the others: "Oh, he's far too valuable for that." May the Lord spare me from being so favored.

The shape of this world, if there had been no horses, cannot be imagined; it has been only a paltry eighty or ninety years since everything, but everything, relied on their muscles and bones. I look out my window onto land being reclaimed minute by minute, it seems, by the maples and oaks, but which once was completely cleared of them by horses. I sit in a house whose foundation is made of stone gathered by horses and whose wood frame consists of boards felled, cut, and then hauled here using horses. My car over there is rated still by horsepower.

To be so necessary, so adaptable, so gentle, useful, resilient, easy-keeping, valiant, strong, leads to being exalted. "Hast thou clothed his neck with thunder? Canst thou make him leap as a locust? The glory of his nostrils is terrible. He paweth in the valley, and rejoiceth in his strength: he goeth on to meet the armed men. He mocketh at fear, and is not affrighted; neither turneth he back from the sword. The quiver rattleth against him, the glittering spear and the shield. He swalloweth the ground with fierceness and rage: neither believeth he that it is the sound of the trumpet.

He saith among the trumpets, Ha, ha; and he smelleth the battle afar off, the thunder of the captains, and the shouting." Thus the Book of Job; a somewhat more recent sentiment, from James Whitcomb Riley, is titled "The Hoss":

> *Love the Hoss from hoof to head,*
> *From head to hoof and tail to mane*
> *I love the Hoss, as I have said,*
> *From head to hoof and back again.*
>
> *I love my God the fust of all,*
> *Then him that perished on the Cross;*
> *And next my wife and then I fall*
> *Down on my knees and love the Hoss.*

"Thou shalt fly without wings . . ." The human heart, too, flies on viewing its divine companion, in awe of this gift of power so freely given. Tears fall at the sight of such grace. Only elevation to immortality in myth (Bucephalus, Pegasus, the holy unicorn) suits it. And only a reality of opposite kind marks it as belonging to us.

To be so necessary, so adaptable, so gentle, useful, resilient, easy-keeping, valiant, strong, leads to being aggrieved and agonized without conscience. Great Britain was known prior to this century as "the Hell of horses," but it is hard to know why it should have been singled out. In 1533 Laurentius Rusius wrote in *Hippiatrica Sive Marescalia* of the proper way to train a difficult horse:

> The nappy horse should be kept locked in a stable for forty days, thereupon to be mounted wearing large spurs and a strong whip; or else the rider will carry an iron bar, three or four feet long and ending in three well-sharp-ened hooks, and if the horse refuses to go forward he will dig one of these hooks into the horse's quarters and draw him forward . . . an assistant may apply a heated iron bar under the tail while the rider drives the spurs in with all available strength.

History's other remedies for the recalcitrant mount include a cat or hedgehog tied to the tail, being plow-yoked by the tail, all manner of caustics applied in all manner of places, use of bits made of spikes or with such long sidepieces that a small amount of pressure could break the horse's jaw, training aids consisting of boards with protruding nails; the modern age has brought the expected refinements, largely in the form of electricity and drugs, but modifications of the former are still also widely used.

What could be termed the unavoidable side effects of the traditional work to which horses were put were hardly less deleterious. Certainly the numbers they affected were greater. Only recently did it come to notice, for instance, that the harness used in Sumeria, Chaldea, ancient Egypt, Greece, Rome, and throughout the Western world (only China was exempt) well past the tenth century was the "inefficient" throat-and-girth type that caused the horse to self-suffocate with every step, by pulling against his own trachea.

Then there was, inevitably, war. The toll of horse life on the battlefields of human wars can hardly be conceived. With Napoleon in Russia, one division lost 18,000 of 43,000 mounts in the space of two months; in the 1812 retreat from Moscow, 30,000 horses died, mainly from cold and privation. The Peninsular War caused Wellington to call the Peninsula "the grave of horses": the 14th Light Dragoons alone lost 1,564 horses (of 1,840 total), while their loss of men was 654. The Boer War cost the lives of some 500,000 horses, mules, and donkeys (the Australians shot all their surviving Walers over the age of twelve when the war ended, since they couldn't be returned home due to quarantine restrictions). In World War II, Germany lost an average of 865 horses per day over the war's two thousand days—52,000 in the Battle of Stalingrad alone. (Entire libraries of books are written about this war without any mention of the millions of animals who perished.) One day in 1939 the Pomeranian Cavalry Brigade lost 2,000 horses in thirty minutes; a witness described the road to Warsaw as lined with thousands of dead and dying horses. The annihilating charge of the Polish cavalry against German Panzer tank divisions stands today as the very emblem of grotesque futility. You will note that this very partial accounting begins only with the nineteenth century.

A place less conducive than a war to the horse's biological nature—possessing extreme sensitivity to sound, smell, and touch; a prey animal highly tuned to potential danger even should it appear on the distant horizon—cannot be envisioned, unless it is to picture the interior of a coal mine.

Pit ponies were used to haul track carts inside the black and dusty holes, and never did they see the light of day. Forty-two thousand were worked to death in Great Britain's mines, where they continued in use until 1971. In *Germinal*, Émile Zola described the place from the pony's point of view:

> Soon Trompette was lying on the iron flooring, an inert mass. Still he did not move, but seemed lost in the nightmare of this black and endless cavern, this vast chamber full of noises. As they were setting about untying him, up came Bataille, who had just been unharnessed. He stretched his neck and sniffed at this new pal who had dropped down from the earth. . . . Perhaps he found in his new friend the good smell of the open air, the long-forgotten smell of the sun-kissed grass, for all of a sudden he burst into a resounding whinny, a song of joy with a sob of wistfulness running through it. This was his act of welcome, made up of delight in this fragrance of the old, far-off things and sadness that here was one more prisoner who would never go back alive.

While some may have found these particular animals worthy of pity, fewer felt it for the millions of equines in plain view carrying on with daily work, perhaps because if pity were to be felt for some, all would soon demand it, and life would clang to a halt. Every city, town, and village was clogged with horses pulling delivery wagons, refuse carts, carriages, traps and coaches, fire engines and streetcars and ambulances. The year 1916 saw fifty thousand of them dead in New York City's streets.

In 1866 Henry Bergh formed the American Society for the Prevention of Cruelty to Animals, modeled after Britain's Royal Society for the Prevention of Cruelty to Animals, which had been founded in 1824. Both groups were concerned primarily with the treatment of horses, since they were by far the most visible victims of abuse; Bergh had been inspired when he witnessed the beating of a downed cart horse in St. Petersburg, and the ASPCA's emblem shows the hand of an angel of mercy staying the whip of a driver intent on lashing his prone horse. In 1877 Anna Sewell published *Black Beauty,* the first-person tale of the ever-declining fortunes of a carriage horse and some of his confreres, a book she conceived of not as children's literature but as instruction for carriage drivers. Despite being billed in America "The 'Uncle Tom's Cabin' of the Horse"—and ultimately becoming the sixth best-selling book in the English language—its plaint did not sufficiently reach, or make the desired effect on, its intended audience. In part this was because *Black Beauty* soon became known as a children's book, and children did not drive delivery wagons or fancy carriages. Moral concern for animals has long been considered the sole province of children, something to be grown out of eventually, and one probable reason is that we thus avoid having to sacrifice the expediences that make daily life economical. The book's message was largely ignored (except, perhaps, toward the eventual abandonment of the brutal fashion for the bearing rein), and only changing times—in the form of the horse's messiah, the internal combustion engine—would much improve the equine's lot. This is reflected in an unusually feeling editorial published in New York's *Independent* on February 23, 1914:

> As we look down on Broadway from our eyrie we see a cheering sight. The street is blocked with vehicles so that it looks like a log-jam in a mountain canyon. Jack Frost, the arch-enemy of all civilization, has visited us in the night and skilfully prepared the way so as to delay and endanger the traffic as much as possible. First, he glazed the pavement with a thin hard coating of ice, then he cov-

ered and concealed it with a layer of powdered snow a foot deep. Thru this the horses flounder, straining at the tugs, twisting this way and that, their heads tossing, their mouths frothing at the irritating jerks of the bits, the skin on their flanks quivering under the repeated strokes of the whip-lash in the hands of the angry driver. The animals are for the most part doing their best to stir the clogged wheels, but here is one which has given up and laid down on its side, preferring to die in the soft snow bed rather than keep on. There is another whose feet have slipt to either side, leaving him sprawled helplessly. And there is a horse, a trim high-bred creature, downed for keeps, apparently with a broken leg.

It is, as we say, a cheering sight, comparatively speaking, for there are only three horses down and not more than a dozen altogether in the street. A few years ago we might have seen fifty horses, straining and struggling in the snow.

WHAT A STRANGE DUALITY to persist and flourish, capable of sprouting only in the human mind: one animal, at once supremely valued and beneath contempt. This story of burnished love cannot be torn from what is written on the back of the page, under the shadow of a darkness we wish not to explore in ourselves and so wish not to see in our doings.

THERE ARE THOSE who feel abjectly grateful to have been born in the second half of the twentieth century, and in one of those parts of the world, where machines have replaced animals as pullers and haulers. Now they have only to avoid the parts of town where the tourist carriages go, where they would watch with sick hearts the happy people being pulled along by a creature whose misery shone clearly in his eye, and in his lame step which brings him closer by circles to the end in a slaughter that has been envisioned for him all along. They keep the knowledge quiet inside that a daily confrontation with such cruelty and ignorance, slavery and agony, would have been like a slow drowning. Finally, these emotional defectives, reviled by normal men with a better sense of reality as sentimental fools, would sink forever below the waves of sanity. They imagine their own ends as something very much like Nietzsche's: dispatched into lunacy by the sight of one last beaten horse. Like him, they would have to be pried off the neck of the beast they wished to save, while people gathered to watch with distaste the sight of someone becoming less than human before their very eyes.

"A Familiar Friend."

4

SUNRISE

I T STARTS SOMEWHERE, but just try to find it. Perhaps the truth is buried in the journals of developmental psychology, where it is substantiated that something biologically ordained occurs at around the age of four in a female human's life, some stirring of cells and chemicals that manifests in a sudden obsession with ponies. (Science is silent on the subject of why ponies and not dogs, deer, or sheep.) Children are said to have a poor grasp of real time, but when six-year-old after six-year-old, nine-year-old after nine-year-old, tell you they know exactly when they began loving horses—*It was when I was four: when I saw a pony at a fair, at a neighbor's, in a picture book*—the recurrence of the precise age is noteworthy at least.

Perhaps it should all be filed under "anticipatory coping," the official term for a precrush crush, where a girl practices for the main event, attraction to boys. But I don't think so. The evidence is not with the psychologists on this one. Otherwise, what to make of all the girls who never stop loving horses, even as they begin to cast a desirous eye on others of their own species? Or those for whom this love persists through the years alongside all the other loves—children, parents, spouse, friends—never diminishing, just like those? Anyway, as a concept it sounds a bit suspicious, a construct made of equal parts wishful thinking and threatened manhood: It isn't *real,* that deep pull you feel toward a giant brown beast with sweet breath and soft lips; it's just a rehearsal for the day you meet your true destiny—men.

When I told the other girls at summer camp that my middle initial stood for "Horse," not one of them raised an eyebrow; I personally believed there was a distinct odor of foreordination emanating from my birth sign, Sagittarius, a creature equally man and horse. Surely at camp I did nothing to discourage the impression that nothing else was worth living for, despite the fact that the place was meant to provide an "all-around camping experience," including mandatory swimming lessons in a frigid lake first thing in the morning. (And why not the afternoon? Ask the higher-ups, who delighted in gathering the campers together when someone had been discovered harboring bottled drinking water from home because the camp's water tasted of rotten eggs and made the universal camp libation known as bug juice earn the appellation with shocking similitude. The offending girl would be made to dump the water on the grass publicly to the accompaniment of a rousing speech about the value of toughing it out and foregoing special favors that could not be shared by all.) One morning I could not face my thighs turning blue one more time and told the counselors I was sick and could not swim. I made it early, therefore, to the ten-thirty riding lesson, and I spent my time whispering sweet nothings to my chosen, who was named Esmeralda. But I was discovered before I could mount, and a pointing finger directed me back to my cabin. "If you're too sick to swim, you're too sick to ride." I saw it would have done no good to assert the obvious, that one can never be too sick to ride, and so I repaired to my bed and cried for hours. Thereafter ice water was simply the price to pay for an hour on horseback, and in terms of exchange it really didn't seem that steep.

One woman tells me her story, a far better one, since she was informed as a girl that she *was* a horse. She first rode at one, and competed at six. Her parents, she said, trained a dog and a horse to take care of her when she was barely walking, and she has pictures of herself as an infant crawling among the long legs of animals. Now she says it feels ungainly, strange, when she walks the earth on her own legs—only on a horse can she feel truly graceful.

JEANA YEAGER, THE PILOT who with Dick Rutan flew the first glider to circumnavigate the globe, writes in her memoir, *Voyager:*

> My first spoken sentence was "I want a horse." . . . When I was four we moved from Fort Worth to Garland, just north of Dallas. . . . I would take my toy horses and scramble up into [a wisteria vine] and be lost in play there for hours. . . . When we moved to Oxnard, California . . . the wisteria was replaced as my hideaway by a little attic room. . . . I laid out all my toys in order. My palomino horses were all together; the grays, blacks, whites, and sorrels were all together, and each group was arranged according to sizes and names. Even if I was blindfolded I could retrieve any one of them.

I am wondering if memories this specific, this alive years later, could be about anything else.

A HORSE CALLED WONDER—written by "Joanna Campbell," no doubt the pen name of a consortium of underpaid ghostwriters—is the first in the "Thoroughbred" series of Young Adult paperbacks, starring young Ashleigh Griffin. The cover shows her sitting in a stall with a broodmare looking protectively over her while she cradles the head of a newborn foal and offers it a baby bottle. Since nothing gets done in this corner of the publishing world without ample market research, you can be sure the scene represents fantasy fulfillment for what is considered a significant share of young female readers.

The character of the heroine needs to be instantly established in the first few pages of such a book, and is usually conveyed using symbolic shorthand. So here Ashleigh is described most quickly as what she is not—like her sister. "While Ashleigh had raced around on her pony, Caroline had sat in the backyard reading a book or experimenting with nail polish." Or, as the fine print between the lines has it: "Girlie stuff—yuck!"

Recall another instance when nail polish formed a similar borderline between the horsey girl and the girlie girl. In *National Velvet,* Velvet's older sister paints her nails (and little brother Donald's, too). This is how we know, in one image, that she is unlikely to become a true heroine, one who prevails against odds—and gender—and marks herself unique among girls.

And at some point the book will reveal the key. It will animate the dream. You may not be aware that you are reading anything but another sentence deployed as are all the sentences, as a brick that builds a story. But its placid surface parts to show you the truth— although it sounds too bloody *simple* to be the truth at the heart of such a long and large mystery. "Ashleigh didn't think horses were as dumb as some people thought. You just had to understand them and get them to love and trust you—then they behaved beautifully." Remember these words: *understand, love, trust.* Then you will know something of the truth. Not all of it, because truth never permits itself to be known all at once, as you well know. But you will know something of the seed from which it grows.

THERE IS MORE. Another motif, another part of what we might call the truth. There is the underprivileged girl for whom horses represent an unattainable, enticing dream of freedom and beauty, which is set off from the daily reality of urban poverty. Such is the setup in *Not on a White Horse,* a 1988 novel by Nancy Springer, in which Rhiannon DiAngelo lives in a hard-up coal-mining town in Pennsylvania with her unemployed drunkard of a father.

The theme of imagining horses in a suburban setting—in other words, in having them where it is impossible to have them—salves a powerfully persistent ache. Thus, in this book, Rhiannon discovers a whole herd of horses down a road marked NO TRES-PASSING, and, in the mode of the fantasy nonpareil, a nice owner who insists they "need to be ridden." The same stock figure surfaces in *National Velvet,* but, then, virtually every aspect of preadolescent horse worship was engraved in Enid Bagnold's book and thus nothing can be new. (The man who commits suicide leaves his horses to the extremely poor Velvet, the fantasy being that someone can *see* how much you love horses and will simply give them to you—a return to the Edenic world of infancy, when mother observed, interpreted expression, and fulfilled needs, all without having to be asked.)

Imagining horses in a suburban setting is about imagining nature into existence, in one motion wiping away what is there and replacing it with something better, something anterior, something more primitive: horses. With them you rearrange the world to your liking.

THERE'S THE CLICHÉ—girls and horses, eh? wink, wink—and then there's the anticliché cliché—no, it's *really* about little girls empowering themselves. You know, they get to steer around thousand-pound animals and feel on top of things for a change. But girls feel about as invincible when the cake comes out of the Suzy Homemaker bake oven just perfect. For every oversimplification there is a corresponding complication. Rarely, thank goodness, is it anything like in the movie *International Velvet,* a bloodless sequel to *National Velvet* in which Velvet's niece (a sullen Tatum O'Neal) becomes a rider for the British Equestrian Team in the Olympics.

One unintentionally (I think) humorous scene has young Sarah Brown discovering she's been given the colt she covets, and animal and girl race toward one another in slow motion, a reference to that old commercial in which sexual ecstasy is suggested by the delayed conjoining of a man and a woman running to meet in a similar flower-studded field.

And so boys may not compete on equal footing with horses in girls' desires, but horses do not substitute for them, either; if the generic literature is to be trusted as representative, then girls want a whole mess of things all at once: parental understanding, one special boy, *and* a horse of their own. Of course, the boy needs to be a horsey boy. Exemplary in this genre is Patricia Calvert's *The Stone Pony* (1982), in which JoBeth learns to mourn her dead sister, ride her sister's horse, and receive the affection of a boy named Luke.

The true intricacy of feminine desire may well be best captured in the slogan for a British toy series called My Beautiful Horses. Defining the three pillars of girlhood, they are "To Groom, Care For & Collect." There you have it. Indeed these models provide plenty to groom, for their fancifully colored manes and tails sweep the ground, like those of the counterpart American pony that comes with brushes and barrettes.

But all love is at base sexual, or at base social, or perhaps even deeper at base the social *is* sexual, and since we don't know where these things begin and end in our daily life, we are not about to demarcate them when it comes to girls and horses, either. More than one mother has described the relationship with her baby as the greatest love affair of her life, and to bury your face in your child's stomach, to breathe its peculiar odor, to crave its touch, to fear distance, are both so common and so reminiscent of sexual desire that we hardly need go on. Walter Farley's classic *The Black Stallion,* in which a boy manages to tame the madly untamable using only his patient heart, succeeds so perfectly because it is the stripped-down essence of two key horse-love themes: mutual rescue, and the ultimate fantasy (which mutates to accommodate any suitable object of desire)—shipwrecked on an uninhabited island together!

In domesticating horses, we have simultaneously infantilized them to the point that they require constant care. The more removed from their natural sphere, the more dependent they become—needing to be fed, groomed, and their shit taken away on a schedule that rivals the newborn baby's. Thus into our relationship with them necessarily venture issues of nurturance, love, desire, control, and all the attendant complications, as well as analogs for every aspect, of human relationships. So it is not surprising to find, among current representations of the horse, a subset that could only be called horse porn—luscious color magazine centerfolds, suitable for pinning up; calendars sporting a different breed each month; collectible plates and sweatshirt paintings with impossibly proud stallions testing the dark wind and bearing titles like "Spirit of the Mist."

I DO NOT RECALL exactly when I met my fate in the look of a horse. Perhaps it was at the Fourth of July celebration we always attended at the home of friends of my parents: They had a horse farm. She was a noted authority on Morgans and, later, Thoroughbreds, and an author of many books about horses, and a woman I came to admire and fear as if they were the same thing when I first started taking lessons there. I was taught by one of her employees (each female) but was always looking for her so that I could watch out of the corner of my eye as she worked with horses or more advanced students. But in the beginning I just remember the annual summertime blast, with what seemed to me, and perhaps was, hundreds of guests, children running everywhere, galvanized water troughs filled with ice and soda and beer, and the Rubber City Retreads playing Dixieland. We would give the Shetland pony beer, and we would ride her; her name was Black Beauty. For a time I loved her.

5

COMP LIT

CONFIDANT

Those happy days of going for a horseback ride every day after school had been so short-lived. Bucky-B always behaved for her. Of course, she had taken it slow and easy, talking to him in a low friendly voice and making sure always to have an apple or carrot in her pocket, or maybe a handful of oats. She'd learned that trick when getting acquainted with Patches, her pony, whom she had outgrown and traded in as part-payment for Bucky-B. Now spiders busily spun webs in Bucky's stall.

Pushing the shed door open, Lori slipped inside. Hands on hips, she stared at the battered blue bike. What good was a bike? You couldn't talk to it or pet it or feed it or win it for a friend.

—*Pounding Hooves*
by Dorothy Grunbock Johnston, 1976

There was something about Lucky Lady that appealed to her. It had been that way from the beginning. It was still that way as she listened to her history. She felt a kinship with this horse who had been through so much. She had seen that latent excitement boiling up in Lucky Lady, and she felt that somehow it was like a seething something inside herself—a yearning to be understood, a wanting to realize herself as an individual. "She's a little like me," she thought.

—*Three Loves Has Sandy*
by Amelia Elizabeth Walden, 1955

All of a sudden she wished that she could climb up on Harlequin's manger and talk it all over with him while playing with that lush red mane and foretop, or slip the saddle on him and have a quiet ride down their old back road. The feeling was so intense as to be almost physical but she dared not give in to her impulse.

—*Bluegrass Champion*
by Dorothy Lyons, 1949

BOND

She patted Frosty just behind the saddle, and he turned around and looked at her, his face gentle, and mousy, and perpetually surprised. She flicked him gently with a leafy switch. She understood, now, how much you could love one horse.

—*Hobby Horse Hill*
by Lavinia R. Davis, 1939

"Come—come—come," called Jane, holding out her hands. "Why Bells—Wrangle, where are your manners? Come, Black Star—come, Night. Ah, you beauties! My racers of the sage!"

Only two came up to her; those she called Night and Black Star. . . . The first was soft dead black, the other glittering black, and they were perfectly matched in size, both being high and long-bodied, wide through the shoulders, with lithe, powerful legs. That they were a woman's pets showed in the gloss of skin, the fineness of mane. It showed, too, in the light of big eyes and the gentle reach of eagerness.

—*Riders of the Purple Sage*
by Zane Grey, 1912

BLOOD

She never grazed so contentedly as when Judy stood close beside her and rested her hand on her shoulders or withers. These hours spent together were a joy to the young girl for horses were in her blood.

—*Afraid to Rid*
by C. W. Anderson, 1957

But sometimes a wave of homesickness broke over her with such force that she didn't know how she could stand it. That was when she *had* to talk about horses . . . the horses she had known and loved, the ones she was going to have when she was old enough to work and have a ranch of her own again. Horses were "in her blood," as Uncle Joe said.

—"If Wishes Were Horses"
by Adele De Leeuw, 1955

Her grandfather smiled, a broad white smile in the middle of his tanned, lined face. "You've got horses in your blood, Janet. Don't let anyone tell you otherwise."

—*Night Mare*
by Vicki Kamida, 1997

SMELL

Racing into the brick-paved stable yard, still glistening wet from the dew, she could hear them stamping and pawing restlessly as they awakened; she could smell them, too, and she drew in the deepest breath she could hold, filling her nostrils with the wonderful, exhilarating stable smell of sweet hay and ammonia and warm, strong life . . . *horses!*

—*The Horsemasters*
by Don Stanford, 1957

Carole sat deeply into the saddle, moving forward and back with the horse's motions. She loved almost everything about riding, but it was hard to think of anything more fun than cantering gently across an open field on a graceful horse like Diablo, with the bright, warm sunshine beaming down from above. The tangy smell of the hay in the meadow blended perfectly with the rich smell of horses and leather. Carole was content.

—*The Saddle Club No. 5: Trail Mates*
by Bonnie Bryant, 1989

CHARMED

As she put her arm around his neck, Snake Dancer rumbled to a halt. His sides were heaving, his nostrils flared, and his sensitive ears were flat back, but he stood still for *her*. Not for the men in uniforms, not for the man who had come from behind them—a big man in a cowboy hat. For *her*.

—*A Horse for X.Y.Z.*
by Louise Moeri, 1977

A strange calm washed through her as Big Tex wheeled, a startled whinny breaking in his throat. She drew herself up to her full height. Again she sent her call down to him, clear and unbroken in the silence. This time she waved.

Big Tex's eye caught the movement and he broke toward her with a sharp, joyful cry. Eternity seemed spun into that second to Jan. And then he was there, whimpering softly. She slipped her arm up around his blood-streaked neck and pressed her cheek tearfully against his soft, quivering muzzle.

—"Big Tex"
by Pat Follinsbee, 1948

But the wind was not hot and burning; it was cool, and the hands were not the boy's hands. They were the hands of the girl who loved him, who had stayed beside him when he felt so hot and tired he didn't want to stand up, when he found he couldn't stand up. He remembered her hands moving over his aching body, reassuring him. The huge ravine gaped open before him, and the girl was driving him toward it, asking him, trusting him, loving him. He took a firmer hold of the bit and did not hesitate.

—*A Horse Called Holiday*
by Frances Wilbur, 1992

"He's killed two men," I said, "and I'm going to shoot him." I expected her to cry. Her eyes were wide, bright with tears, and her lower lip trembled. Instead she picked up the coffeepot, threw it at me and ran straight for the stables. Wiping the coffee out of my eyes I followed her. By the time I had got onto the stoep she had reached Crusader's box and opened the door.

The horse was screaming with excitement as he saw her. When she got him outside, instead of galloping off, he stood. With a flying jump she was across his back, her left hand on his mane. She wriggled forward and got her right leg over him. Then she slapped him with her open hand and they were off, tearing across the veld, her yellow hair flying behind her all mixed up with Crusader's mane as she leaned over his neck.

—"Crusader
by Stuart Cloete, 1943

RESCUE

A terrible gust of wind whipped the branches of a tree against my face. I realized then exactly what I would have to do. Without my weight Cirque stood a chance of crossing the river. But he would have to be driven forcibly into the water. I leaned as far forward as I could and screamed at Wake, "Catch Cirque's tail!"

—"A Touch of Arab"
by Vivian Breck, 1949

The trot broke into a gallop. Janice urged him on faster, and Brown Beauty stretched out. It was swift, easy running, smooth, flowing speed. This was not mad, frenzied racing such as Martin had forced him to. This was deliberate, willing running.

. . . They came to the dusty little town of Coleville and

Janice reined the horse in sharply before Dr. Crandell's office.

—"Brown Beauty"
by W. T. Person, 1940

She dashed over to him and caught his bridle. He tossed his head and sidled away from her, prancing with excitement. As she talked quietly to him, with swift fingers she loosened the longe, letting it fall to the ground. She felt sure that she could guide him if only she could get on him and stay on him when he bolted. She thrust her hand deep in her pocket and brought out two of the sugar lumps she had been saving for him.

"Sugar for a good boy," she panted and reached up to his muzzle.

—"The Winning of Dark Boy"
by Josephine Noyes Felts, 1945

WANT

There were only two things that she would spend money on; one was movies which had horses in them (and she saw all of those) and riding lessons at Helen's. Mostly she was able to get her dad or her mother to pay for the riding lessons but sometimes she could not, and then she very reluctantly tapped the fund. By that year when she was thirteen, she had almost one hundred dollars.

That was the year she began to grow tall. She had been a chubby little thing earlier, but suddenly she began to shoot up and all her hems were let out in a desperate effort to keep her properly clothed. I had expected she would be displeased at this sudden shooting upward, but I found her philosophical.

"It's much easier to mount now, Uncle Red."

The fourteenth year was when the pin-up boy appeared on her wall.

"It made me feel old," Joe said. "Here was my daughter starting to put up boys' pictures. It made me feel darned peculiar. So when the time was right I said to her, 'I was in your room today, Jeanie, and I noticed that Roy Rogers is your pin-up boy.' And she said, 'Oh, Daddy, that isn't Roy Rogers' picture. That's a picture of Trigger, his horse.' "

—"No Sum Too Small"
by Murray Hoyt, 1947

6

BACK STORY

I N "A CHAPTER FOR Young Women" in *The People's Home Medical Book* of 1915, T. J. Ritter, M.D., advises girls who have just come of age that "Outdoor exercise is the best" and, of the possibilities, that "Horse back riding is good and also the taking care of a horse, cleaning, feeding him, etc. This is a very good and a valuable aid curing girls who have chlorosis." Since medical knowledge was then, as it appears to be today, often at great odds with itself (not to mention with actuality), another manual of the same era says that riding is dangerous to female anatomy: It produces "an unnatural consolidation of the bones of the lower body, ensuring a frightful impediment to future functions which need not here be dwelt upon."

Of course, no one paid the slightest attention to either suggestion, again continuing to do as culture, tradition, and personal desire decreed. And so women have ridden horses, if not quite loved them with late-twentieth-century fervor, for millennia.

A bit of news that should have been conveyed to all those teams that until recently barred women players is that polo was originally played by females, in ancient Persia and China. They apparently did all right, too, if the Persian poet Nisami (1140–1202) can be believed:

> Seventy girls rode out onto the field in fervent ardor before their queen. In courage each one was like the Isfardiar, in their skill with the bow they were equal to the knights and they played polo so well that they played as when the sun rises and a falcon swoops down to catch a partridge.

But of course they did all right. Riding is merely like flying or motorcycling or target shooting, in that female proficiency must be a matter of established record for several hundred years or the equivalent before it can be officially permitted, grudgingly and under duress. And precedents be damned, even if they are of ancient vintage. In the fourteenth century, Knighton (the name given in an 1857 book) described women of great beauty who wore tunics, small caps, and daggers, and who "are mounted on the finest horses, with the richest furniture, and in this attire they ride about from place to place in quest of tournaments." Because it is not known if they are myth or were real, let us leave aside the subject of the Amazons, even if we do allow ourselves to pause to recall that they kept men around only for purposes of procreation and slavery.

Back in the land of the durably real, there is the example of Elizabeth (Libbie) Custer, wife of the general, who was a daring sort, even to be with her husband on the wild and lonely Plains in the late nineteenth century. He wrote of her to her father:

Libbie . . . is now an expert horse-woman, so fearless she thinks nothing of mounting a girthless saddle on a strange horse. [Such might have caused second thoughts for her husband, who was a decidedly mediocre horseman.] You should see her ride across the Texas prairies at such a gait that even some of the staff officers are left behind.

Flying along the surface of the earth is a simple pleasure, irreducible and without peer, magnetic for that simplicity. To borrow the power of another to achieve something so near to pure freedom without its becoming final death is an intoxication. This must be what Catherine Cavender, a late-nineteenth-century Kansan, meant when she described her early life with exclamation: "Our joys were horseback rides! Wild dashes across the prairie, the wind painting our cheek with nature's red!" Health benefits are one thing, but ecstasy is quite another.

And so is a loosening of constraints, social or physical or both. The American West offered opportunities for this pleasurable relief that were lacking in the East. Thus Joe (or Jo) Monaghan set out for Montana from New York in 1867, dressed as a man. She worked at silver mining and sheepherding before turning to bronc busting, at which she developed such skill that upon her death in 1903 the *Boise City Capital News* was moved to declare, "No horse was too wild or savage that he could not be brought to saddle and butt under Little Jo's hands." It is possible that she performed in a Wild West show, bringing her into company with at least sixteen women known to have competed against men in rodeos or shows at that time; they were among the first American women to become professional athletes. Rough around the cultured edges as the West was wont to be, it could not have been easy for them, and indeed excuses to exclude women were often sought. The most successful turned out to be the death of bronc rider Bonnie McCarroll, thrown and trampled to death at the 1929 Pendleton Round-Up Rodeo. The event's organizers voted thereafter to ban women, notwithstanding the fact that plenty of men had been killed at rodeos without incurring a similar response. That year the

Rodeo Association of America was formed and, perhaps not unco-incidentally, did not encourage or sanction women's events. So women took it upon themselves to form the Girls Rodeo Association in 1948 (to reflect changing sentiments, it was renamed the Women's Professional Rodeo Association in 1982).

Similar battles have been fought, and continue to pervert peace, in the arena of professional racing, and since more money is at stake, the war is all the bloodier. Sometimes literally. Women jockeys have had rocks thrown through their windows, their horses smashed to the rail, and, in at least one instance, a whip lashed across the face. They have been boycotted and jeered. And all this by the men who, in seeking reasons to bar women from the track, initially proposed that since it is men's instinct to protect women from harm, the dangers into which they would naturally and continually fall would keep men so busy being chivalrous, it would prevent them from doing their job. ("There is hazard in playing a man's role in handling the spirited thoroughbred horses. But narrow escapes from death have not deterred Mrs. Hubbard" from her work as a trainer and trader, darkly asserted *The American Magazine* in 1930 about one early breaker of boundaries.) Closer to the truth is the raw fear revealed by a jockey who in the late sixties was quoted as saying, "If you let one woman ride in one race, we're all dead."

That fear was greatly exaggerated; furthermore, a knowledge of history could have prevented his anxiety. In 1804 in England, the first battle of the sexes had already been played out over four miles of racecourse. The upstart was twenty-two-year-old Alicia Meynell, who had a weighty bet of fifteen hundred pounds riding on her back. Her opponent queered the start by bumping her horse and taking off, and though the young lady—and let us not forget to mention her mount—took the lead for three miles, she pulled her fading horse up before crossing the finish. Her backer refused to make good on his bet. The next year she found another jockey willing to face the potential humiliation of losing to a woman, and it was a good thing that he was, since he did.

It was in the 1950s—again, coinciding with the final banish-

ment of horses from military and economic centrality—that numbers of women tried to get jobs at racetracks. You can imagine the
sort of rebuff, and its usual delicacy. But as they began to succeed,
trainers acknowledged that they might have been missing something all along: "The biggest things she has going for her are
patience and a genuine fondness for horses most men just don't
have," said one in Larry Adler's *Young Women in the World of Race
Horses;* another added, "Our horses seem to respond better to girls
than men. I don't know why, but the horses seem to sense the love
the girls have for them. . . . We noticed an improvement in the disposition of many of our horses when they were being groomed by
a girl rather than a man." When coupled with evidence by now
well out of the fluke range that women jockeys and trainers are at
least the equal of men, logic would dictate that racing would be
replete with women, if not completely dominated by them. That
this is far from the case is just one more proof, if anyone was looking for one, that we are not logical animals. Only one impetus to
behavior seems more powerful than money, and that is aversion to
change. This would explain why Beryl Markham, the pilot and
author of *West with the Night* and possessor of the first trainer's
license given to a woman in Africa, had a promising horse taken
from her and given to a male trainer, despite the fact that her capabilities were to give her no fewer than six Kenya Derby winners.
Because nothing else *could* explain it.

MAYBE ONE COULD SEE it as a sort of latter-day Feast of
Misrule, to have reached a time when pursuing an activity that was
being derided as regressive around the turn of the century has
become an act of feminism. Whether women should ride astride
or aside was a subject of much sweat-spraying debate a hundred
years ago. In 1910 a Georgia legislator proposed a bill that would
make it unlawful for a woman to ride upon what was known as a
cross saddle—unless she should be a circus performer, and everyone knew that *their* kind was already operating outside the bounds
of decency. So as not to upset King Edward with such an untoward

sight, women riding astride were prohibited from Hyde Park's Row when the royal was there. And the editorials were flung down like gauntlets. "If the side-saddle is best for rider and horse, why do not men wear skirts and use it?" asked one in 1899; an even more strongly worded article in 1901 by Elizabeth Yorke Miller in *Munsey's Magazine* pointed out, "Should woman ride astride? Well, humanly speaking, why shouldn't she do what she wants to? One never finds men deep in solemn conclave as to whether man should do this or that. Each decides for himself to the best of his lights, and there is no tedious debate on the subject." A response in 1910 opined that "the woman's physiological lines below the waist are not the right conformation to get a good riding grip with the knees." The tedious debate did indeed go on. In 1912 an editor's note appended to an article on the subject in *Country Life* cautioned the reader that "It is well to bear in mind . . . that the one reason side saddles are used by women—and probably always will be—lies in the delicate structure of the woman herself . . . the incontrovertible fact remains, according to physicians, that, taking women in general, their physical organism is not fitted to bear the strain of the position in cross-saddle riding." Finally, by 1923, when *Riding Astride for Girls* was published by Ivy Maddison, the sidesaddle was less visible and less a topic for dispute. "It is a known fact that nothing worthless ever lives," writes the author with excessive optimism, "and since the cross saddle has not only held its own but has been adopted by the majority of girls in this generation, it must possess more merit than was first supposed." It would also obviate the need for such "escorts" as were required by a properly attired lady of previous centuries and described in a 1902 article on "Southern Women Who Ride to Hunt":

> A woman then went forth to hunt with a long, full skirt which almost swept the ground, a short jacket buttoned to the throat, and a hat that would suggest Queen Guinevere as she rode with Lancelot in the youth of the year. A waving plume and gauze veil floating behind completed a

costume most charming, but utterly unsuited to the purpose for which it was designed. Her "escort" in knee
breeches and cocked hat rode on her left, in order to have
his right arm ready to assist in case of the probable turning of her saddle.

But during the hard years when women were forced to accept
these limitations and ride aside, lest they appear "a hoydenish creature with a shocking lack of modesty whose only reason for
adopting [the cross saddle] must be a desire to ape masculine ways
and make herself unduly conspicuous," they created a culture, a
language, a level of attainment, that would be lost like a fossil in
deep layers if not for the efforts of a few unlikely archaeologists.

CENTRAL OHIO IS FLAT. It is very flat. Maps of the area look
like schematic drawings of plaid, the roads are laid out so straight.
And why bother to make them curve when the land is so flat? You
can see where you're going hours before you make it there. As you
drive you can watch your progress mirrored in the everlasting
plow lines of the fields to either side, and every once in a while
you will pass through a town like Bucyrus, with trees and little
brick houses and a Dairy Queen, but not very often. Mostly it's
just flat. But when you reach the crossroads settlement called
Brokensword, you have arrived at the headquarters of the World
Sidesaddle Federation.
    The organization has a Web site, publishes a newsletter titled
Aside World Magazine, and has a library of historical documents
that is open by appointment. All of them are housed on the
upstairs landing, outside the bedroom door, of the small Cape Cod
house belonging to the organization's founder. She is devoted to
keeping alive the traditions of sidesaddle technique, and to this end
the newsletter broadcasts in definitive detail the types of costumes
that reflect verisimilitude—no true "Amazone" ever wore Alice in
Wonderland frilled bloomers under her riding skirt, and the sight
of them at an increasing number of shows these days that include

sidesaddle classes is dim-witted and offensive. It is offensive to the memory of the true skill and seriousness of riders such as Marie Louise Thompson, who, in the early years of the twentieth century, "won 22 successive ladies' jumping classes from Devon to Madison Square Garden and back again. She played polo. She jumped a horse named Confidence over a seven-foot fence in a show at Brockton to establish a world's record that has not yet been equalled by any feminine rider. And she did it all while riding side-saddle." It is also offensive to the notion of true historical preservation and understanding. Lacking respect for that is to give ourselves up to the narcissism of present fantasy, in which everything is brought to the level of historical accuracy of *Doctor Quinn, Medicine Woman*.

The secretary of the World Sidesaddle Federation, who is taking a rest from the July heat on the living room sofa while I peruse the books and files up in the library, consisting of pretty much all the known literature on the subject of sidesaddle, later explains something to me. I am having trouble fitting together Brokensword, Ohio; a technique of riding for ladies of certain social standing that went out, with apparent good reason, seventy years before; and a movement to resuscitate it centered in corn country. It is about saving something that women made, or at least made their own, she says; it is about savoring the power inherent in making oneself feel beautiful and graceful. It is an act of reclamation that becomes an act of celebration: It matters, because we matter. I drove from Brokensword chastened and illuminated, down the long roads of a flat country.

THE MYTHS HAVE BECOME hardened, as dirt compressed for eons becomes rock. And they begin in truth, or what we want to believe is true, both of which sometimes coincide in a miracle: Women are patient, gentle, compassionate; they seem to understand horses, and horses understand them. On horseback, they present "a picture of power over-ruled by gentleness," as the anonymous author (the copy in the Brooklyn library has "Mrs. Stirling (?)

Clarke" handwritten in pencil) of *The Ladies' Equestrian Guide, or, The Habit & the Horse: A Treatise on Female Equitation* put it in 1857. "[T]here is a degree of decision in the hand of a lady accustomed to country life, and who consequently commenced her equestrian exercises in childhood, that becomes a sort of free-masonry between herself and her horse," she goes on. But hear that distant rumbling? It sounds like a train, or danger, when it wants to sneak up on you. This is what I have come to listen to, and for. And so, far from being better or softer trainers, she next points out, some women punish much too quickly and severely, so that the horse forever after associates the sight of a sidesaddle and habit with suffering.

Women are patient, gentle, compassionate. But there is a warning to come. It has even been whispering underneath the pretty valorizations right here. Did you hear it? It was quite soft.

Meeting an Old Friend

7

APPROACH

THE LIBRARY NEAREST our house was at Highland Square, so called even though there was no square and it was merely a part of West Market Street as it headed downtown. This is where my parents would drive me when my need for books, my need for information and transportation away from where I was, grew in pitch to a fatal whine. I suspect now that I had developed an addiction to the smell of binding glue; then, the pervasive scent of the air that pushed at one's face upon pulling the first glass door was simply the ether of excitement. I couldn't believe that this store would let you take home its goods—the best sort of goods, besides penny candy—without paying for them. I could have whatever I wanted, limited only to five per visit.

There might have been books on other subjects there, just as there were no doubt books for adults, but to me it seemed that it was a library of animal books, and there were miniature versions of the sixties-modern wire chairs with orange vinyl seat pads just for me to sit in with a pile of books at my feet. The edges of the pages had been worn to velvet. The specific colors of the pictures are something you never forget. Brown, green. The world I wanted to inhabit was brown and green. Every once in a while it was shot through with yellow.

THE STAPLE OF bad old movies is the heroine whose horse runs away with her, dumps her in a copse of trees, and leaves her moaning to be found and rescued by the (better) male rider. Sometimes he has to try to reach the reins of her runaway in mid-flight as she has become subsumed by her mouth's frozen O of panic.

These scenes elicit an appropriately dismissive snort from the young horsewoman. She knows, from evidence gathered in the stable where she rides, that these roles would more than likely be reversed; she knows, somehow, that the reason so few boys are there is that (as they may grow up to admit much later) they are afraid of horses. At this, too, she would find it hard to curb her derision: Everyone knows that if you show them who's boss from the get-go, a horse is just like wet clay in your hands. What's to be afraid of?

When she turns on the TV it is to watch the horse operas for the horses. Better yet, there are shows like *My Friend Flicka,* in which the people don't step in the way of the horse all the time; even *Mister Ed* is okay, though it hardly does much for the horse's natural dignity (and she has to wonder how they make his lips move like that—looks to her like some form of irritant or wire). But nearly any cowboy picture is made palatable by the mounts. And on *Bonanza* there are even close-ups.

In his memoir *Horses in the Green Valley,* Vian Smith wrote of watching movie horses and what it made him feel:

The small screen of television has taken the place of the Saturday matinee, but the Western persists, as popular with the young as it was to us in the threepennies. The crudities persist also. I'm still offended by the yanking around of horses which seem bewildered or humiliated; still worried by horses which are brought down in the hope of surprising or thrilling somebody. Commercial exploiters of the American myth continue to show little respect for the animal which drew wagons, logged timber, herded cattle; which was for a hundred years man's only means of creating the new out of old wilderness.

I was like Smith, a tender viewer who noticed only the horses in these shows, because they are what mattered. Although they were intended as set dressing, authentic atmosphere, as indistinguishable as the swarms of "Indians," to me they stood out as individuals while it was the handsome white men in hats who receded into a background wall of uniformity. I was enraptured by the way the animals' forelocks flew to one side, admired the plump breasts of muscles, and worried endlessly when they were hauled to a haunch-sitting stop by the long levers of bits that seemed to want to separate the lower jaw from the upper.

MY OLDER SISTER was heading off to Paris for a junior year abroad. We went to celebrate at a French restaurant; happy bon voyage. I was a junior in high school, I ordered beef, steak being one of my favorite things in life. My sister ordered rabbit, to get in the spirit. We laughed and drank wine. I watched her face and wondered what it would feel like to feel such fear and such anticipation, on the eve of a trip into space that might seem as boundless and unknown as it certainly did long, for we were still of an age when a year is as truly inconceivable as the spread of the universe. And all of a sudden I looked at her plate, then at mine, then at hers again. It was possible to see the shape of the animal her dinner had once been, its lean muscles, a striation of white running along curves that locomotion had created. Mine looked like something else, but next to hers the red of the medium rare was reverting to its former self. As it did so my eyes, almost imperceptibly, began to change shape.

That's how it happens, all at once when you don't even want new sight, never asked for it. You try to push it back where it came from, but it won't go. And that's how it is, simple and clean. That was one of the first things.

8

HORSE'S MOUTH

I GREW UP ON a farm near Davis, California, with the joy of my own horse from age five. At that time I learned to shinny up a leg, slide down a tail, and loiter around the horses to my heart's content.

I have been riding since the age of nine and, despite being kicked while trotting by a notorious kicker named Darned Good at Pegasus Stables and breaking my foot, have never really lost my intense love of riding.

I have always been a horse nut, from day one. My parents were both afraid of horses, so it wasn't anything they started or encouraged. Somehow, I was always drawn to these animals. I would beg to go on pony rides at fairs and local events, and even begged my mother to put a quarter in the plastic horse outside the grocery store *every time* we went because, heck, it looked like a horse, and that was enough for me.

As a horse-loving child in the suburbs of Boston, I was reasonably content with riding classes and summer camp where we rode incredibly green, dreadful horses but loved it anyway. I swore then that when I grew up, if a child of mine wanted that pony I so craved, he/she would have it.

There are those who must be with horses. They will do anything to be with horses. I am this way. I went through a typically rough adolescence, my horses being a buffer to the crashing waves of emotions during those years. I rode off bareback into the hills on Breezy, a little bay Hackney mare, so many times to cry or think about some deep problem only had by a teenager.

I became the proverbial barn rat. Between the time I was eleven and the time I was twenty-five I must have worked in ten different barns. I shoveled, brushed, fed, watered, cleaned, and begged, all for the privilege of the occasional free ride or lesson. However, as I neared college age, my family began to steer me in other directions, telling me I was better with my brains than with my brawn and that I'd never make a living training horses, et cetera. All the things that people without that "must be with horses" gene say to convince you that a life working with horses is only a pipe dream.

All those years I'd gravitated to every horse I could get my hands on. After the war we moved to Boston and they let me take riding lessons once a week for a while until we moved again. I was in seventh heaven. I *knew* my destiny.

My mom said I said "horsey" before I could even walk. Every horse I saw I loved. There was no such thing as an ugly horse.

I grew up in Berkeley, California, on a busy street that had not been trod by a horse in over fifty years. I remember the annual parade down Shattuck Avenue in honor of the Cal football team, but to me it only meant . . . horses. Cowboys on horses, Indians on horses, beautiful ladies in harem clothes on horses, and, best of all, horses with glitter on their hooves. When I was about five, our neighbors offered to drive me into town to watch this parade. As I leaped up from the dinner table, my parents reminded me to ask them to wait for my sister Kathie, who was dawdling over her vegetables. In all the excitement, I forgot about Kathie, and spent one enchanted evening gawking at the most beautiful creatures on earth. On the ride home I had a sudden stab of guilt, and dragged myself miserably into the house. Kathie and I shared a bedroom, so there was no escaping her rage. But instead she lay quietly in her bed as I crept into mine, wormlike. Finally she let a little sigh escape, and in a tiny voice she asked, "Were there any palominos?"

They put me aboard and led me down the driveway. I don't know what happened, but I took to it right away.

ALTHOUGH RELATING WITH horses is much like relating with children, the obvious difference is the horse's capability of challenging us physically.

Horses are like children and need a lot of care.

Nothing resembles being in tune with a horse; it's one of life's greatest pleasures. A horse never disappoints. No matter how tough a day you may have had, no matter what problems you think you have, go out and see your horse, and your cares will vanish.

"There's nothing like owning your own horse, honey," he said.

Being able to disappear on my horse for hours on end, unnoticed by my husband, who was lost to the world whenever the football was on, was heaven. I no longer had to worry that I had left him quite long enough and reluctantly turn for home . . . to me the World Cup was sheer bliss.

It is a great love affair.

Gradually, as Pepper and I got closer, he started to trust me more, and eventually we fell in love. Then there was nothing my horse wouldn't do for me.

I bought him off a hack line when he was about six years old. The thought of him belonging to someone else was something I could not accept. Nine years later, I've never looked back. I'm sure he'd walk through fire for me (not that I'd let him!). He is my soul mate. I love him dearly; I could never, ever part with him. My Little Buddy, the light in my life.

She is the delight of my life. She comes running if I call her—if she isn't already standing at the yard gate waiting for me. I am in heaven being able to have her right with me. No matter what happens, that chestnut mare is *there* for me.

Sweeter than any horse I have ever known, Blondie is a true friend.

I had so many adventures and developed such a strong bond with her (especially when riding for seven hours in a torrential thunderstorm, complete with tornados and crashing trees).

And when a hurricane was coming, I begged my mom to let me bring the colt inside, and when she wouldn't I was so mad at her I stayed out in the barn to protect him through the storm.

Yes, he has literally saved my life. Sometimes you ride places so remote there is just the two of you, you depend and rely on each other. You live with them, you eat with them and share your life. Each horse brings different challenges and different joys. They become so much a part of my life and my family that they all stay with my husband and myself after they are retired.

My best friend who saw me through a divorce, a move, new job, all that stuff, was Sam, a huge Plantation walker who liked to be hugged.

The horses (I've had twenty or more) have been the one constant thing in my life. A horse was a father who was never around, a brother or sister I never had. I think, in my mind, the horse could be some sort of anchor for me.

◻

Out at the stable five times a week, I'd spend hours hosing and brushing my horse, braiding his mane and tail, using a pick on his hooves, cleaning his eyes and teeth, lunging and exercising him, feeding him carrots.

◻

Six to eight hours a day in the saddle were pure joy. One experiences the world in that mode, not just sees it.

◻

I always feel good when I am with my horses. No matter how tough the day, even very sad, when I am riding all the world goes away.

◻

I could *not* be happier than when I'm kicking around in the horse manure, smelling like a barn.

◻

My daughter Ryan, at thirteen, lives, breathes (and, sadly, sometimes reeks of) horses.

◻

He is my fetish. I think about him all day. I worship him; he has made me a better person. He has enriched my work: I'm a designer, and everything I do is about creating beauty. He is part of that.

◻

Would he even remember me? After all, it had been three months. It was pitch-dark, close to midnight; nevertheless, the first thing I wanted to do upon deplaning was see my horse. He trembled and bobbed his head up and down, nudged me hard all over my body, licked and lipped me, kept nickering like crazy, shifting his weight, flaring his nostrils, until he finally calmed down a bit, and then he put his head close to mine, breathed softly, warmly, and gently on me, right on my face and into my ear.

I kiss his sweat.

IF MY PARTICULAR PASSION ever kills me, it won't be because I was on a horse's back. It will be because I was gaping out my car window at some horse standing innocently in a field or backyard when I was supposed to be paying attention to the road.

I would much rather buy things for the horses than for myself. I get a lot more excited about looking around the tack shop than going to a clothing store.

I have never, ever regretted getting up at "dark-thirty" in the morning and going up to the barn and feeding horses before I went to work. I love my husband, daughter, and grandsons, and every moment I have ever spent looking at, feeding, riding, cleaning up after, doctoring, hauling around the country, and hugging my horses before I eat breakfast. One rule I've always kept is NO ONE EATS BREAKFAST OR DINNER BEFORE THE HORSES DO!

MY FIRST HORSE was with me until he died at age twenty-nine. My second wonderful gelding (registered Quarter Horse) lived to be twenty-eight. Both are buried out behind the barn with my third husband's thirty-three-year-old mare.

◻

She died at age twenty from severe founder and I buried her in her pasture.

◻

Lost my son (age twenty-seven) ten years ago—cried in my old gelding's mane.

◻

Tiny rarely showed emotion, but once I saw her in Pardita's stall, just leaning against the mare's neck and whispering to her over and over, "I know, I know."

◻

A horse has been called a girl's best friend. So is her mother. They've both been there for me, carrying me on their backs. I look at them now with aching love. I cannot bear to lose them, but I will. They're leaving me.

> *—Jean, Bridget, Lynn, Mary, Martha, Judy,*
> *Jeanne, Donna Fay, Vourneen, Deanne,*
> *Christine, Cheryl, Michelle, Annie,*
> *Virginia, Kerri*

9

PHENOMENAL

H ARD FACTS SEEM in order, some explanation to counteract the huge wash of supposition and, worse, emotion—that which people disdain over science. Am I the only one who suspects something unacknowledged behind this insistence on backup for what the senses already know? Science is often pursued with a fervor that is, well, quite emotional.

But what can I give you to explain this horsey phenomenon? Casual observation? If so, let me tell you that it's real: More than half of all little girls in the industrialized world one sudden day fall madly, truly, deeply in love with horses. Growing numbers of older women one sudden day recall how much they loved horses when they were little girls and decide to call that stable they noticed by the highway the other day, just to go in and walk around, really, nothing serious, but they find themselves talking in a low whisper to a pretty little bay as she methodically and percussively munches her way through two flakes of hay, then they sign up for lessons. The next thing they know, it's back, it's hit them like a gust of wind in the chest, and they've returned whence they came: obsession land, only this time they don't have to whine to a frowning dad to pretty please buy them a pony; now they can buy it for themselves. Now they draw a circle all the way back through the years and realize they have been the same person all along. Now they are complete.

Facts? Of the United States Pony Club's fourteen thousand members, four-fifths are girls. As of 1994, the American Dressage Federation's membership was 95 percent female; other horsemen's groups average out to 65 percent female. A survey taken a few years ago by the British magazine *Gallop!* found that three quarters of women who own horses would as soon give up their husbands as their horses; 90 percent would rather have a new horse than a new baby. The vast majority admitted telling their problems to their equines and not to their partners. Only 22 percent of Canadian horse owners are male.

Now take a less official poll. Why do you, a woman who loves horses, think women love horses?

For one thing, they're a lot like children; we know how to take care of children—it's in our genes.

We don't have anything to prove; we don't need to fix things in order to feel good.

We're more patient, and horses respond best to patience.

You can't use force on a horse, and when many men discover that, they're out of there.

These are not my words. They are words you'll hear again and again and again, out there, if you ask. (One rather unique opinion is that of a ten-year-old: Boys prefer things, like trucks and dinosaurs, you can take home.) These are also not my words:

In disposition the horse is much like a child. Both are governed by kindness combined with firmness; both meet indifference with indifference, but return tenfold in love and obedience any care or affection that is bestowed upon them. The horse also resembles the child in the keenness with which he detects hypocrisy; no pretense of love or interest will impose on either.

They were written by Elizabeth Karr in 1884, in her book *The American Horsewoman*. Since then myriad examples of the truth of her words can be had just for the inquiry: the horse who would not move for the man on his back, no matter how bitter the spur and the whip, but mounted by a woman, in one gentle movement stepped out in grace and ease. Variations on the theme abound.

In acknowledgment of the loving hand, the horse does return at least tenfold to his mistress that which she craves: the banishment of

> melancholy, that dark demon which occasionally haunts even the most joyous life, [which] is overcome and driven back to the dark shades from whence it came. Should the reader have the good fortune to possess an intelligent horse, she can, when assailed by sorrow real or fancied, turn to this true, willing friend, whose affectionate neigh of greeting as she approaches, and whose pretty little graceful arts, will tend to dispel her gloom, and, once in the saddle, speeding along through the freshening air, fancied griefs are soon forgotten, while strength and nerve are gained to face those troubles of a more serious nature, whose existence cannot be ignored.

Or, in a more twentieth-century turn of phrase, that of one woman among many, "Horses are my gin and my therapy."

In fact, the easiest thing in the world, should any researcher desire to undertake it, would be to document the copious riches women derive from their relationships with their equine cohorts. There is the intoxicating sense of power: Give the sign, and off you go; the wind comes up as if you had willed it to blow, while a powerful being who respects your command enough to run without having any other reason to do so pumps so rhythmically beneath you, it is possible to believe you are not two but one. There is the gift of concentration, the shortcut to Zen enlightenment in which the exigencies of the pursuit—pay attention to what's around you, what you are doing with body, mind, breath, *or else*—force you to inhabit the here and the now with a consummate excellence that it would otherwise take you a lifetime to master. There is the opportunity to excel, to learn, to keep pressing on, that is without boundaries (although some believe they meet them every now and then, almost always in the form of their horse or their instructor, never in themselves, and so are always in the market for better equipment). There is someone to talk to, at any hour. There is someone who will cleave unto you, especially since the life of the domesticated horse is so impoverished in the social and intellectual opportunities of his wild counterparts that he has little other choice. Still, even then, perhaps he would prefer you; the tendency to believe that this is so is yet another of the blisses bestowed by the horse.

The many people who have lived in closeness with another animal—a horse or a dog or a cat—are aware that these relationhips are looked upon with unease and even avid disdain by others. They are seen as deficient substitutes for human relationships, signs that one would have really preferred companionship or parenthood of one's own kind but for some faulty functioning in the psyche's wiring. (If that is so, then many other species suffer right along with us: As Professor Frans B.M. de Waal has learned from his extensive studies into animal altruism, "From an evolutionary perspective, care for non-offspring may be maladaptive, but from a psychological perspective, it remains authentic and fitting behavior for the species." Hurrah, say all of those with fur-bearing offspring; science says we are not weird!) But the one who has the relationship already knows that it is no substitute for anything; after all, as the bumper sticker has it, A CHILD IS FOR PEOPLE WHO CAN'T HAVE DOGS. No, it is a fact that the people who look down upon other animals are consigned to live a life in darkness, in the midst of one of the saddest afflictions to which the individual is prey: a lonely narcissism that forever confines one to the stifling hall of mirrors in which no matter where one looks, one sees oneself. For who is more Other than an animal; what can call us forth from the prison of the self better than the need to understand something that is different from us, but which then magically turns to show us how alike we all are?

It is said that children who grow up bilingual are demonstrably smarter than those who are restricted to a world with one language. In terms of interspecies language, it is unfortunately usually animals and not us who permit themselves to benefit from the greater leap in intelligence. I watch my dog listening with cocked ear to my interminable babble of words, hoping to pick out the ones she knows so that she might fulfill the request and receive something she wants. She clearly has a better grasp of my language than I do of hers, so who is the smarter one? It is a miracle that animals have not given up entirely on trying to understand us— we who break the rules of nature even as we are bound to them and thus resent and deny them. Still, their persistent, valiant attempts to do so imply a mutual responsibility: We must also try to understand them. This we can do only by leaving ourselves behind for a time. We must leave our homes and travel abroad, where we will hear whole days of speech we do not comprehend, and witness customs that appear strange and new and possibly repellent. But when we realize that this is also how we appear to the aliens who visit us—what a gift of illumination it is. What a relief to spend some time outside our own tight-fitting clothes. And this is a holiday available only to those who will allow an animal to show them the rest of wide existence and exactly where they are situated inside it.

So it is that horses humanize us. What we do to them we can only guess.

. . .

THEY ARE A MEANS to an end. They are a way to make a living, make a statement, make a killing. They are used to win blue ribbons and to feed the self-renewing lust for such signs of arrival. They connect us back to nature. (No comment.) They are used as a source of never-ending affection and an outlet for our need to give it back. They are helpmeets in biofeedback and physical therapy and self-actualization and quests for what is referred to as spirituality. There is no end to what they give, or to what we ask from them.

We can't seem to keep our hands off animals, even to be "nice"—like the clots of people in the national parks who simply can't help their altruistic urges to feed bits of candy bar to the kaibab squirrels, all the while standing next to signs forbidding one to feed the wildlife. The people can't stop themselves from *giving* to the cutely begging creatures, even though they might as well be beating them with sticks, for all that the squirrels will starve next winter when they come to dig up their worthless cache of spoiled chocolate. Our animal friends *need* us, we think; but it is we who need to feel needed, just as we need to look away from the painful truth that we are but a part, and a minute one at that, of the interlinked world of the other animals. We exist mainly to keep sharp the senses of prey animals, which need to be alert to the dangers we pose. But this does not suit our sense of self-importance, of riding triumphantly to the top of the whole chain of being. What does? The domesticated animal, made dependent on us.

Monty Roberts, the *Man Who Listens to Horses,* was being interviewed by a radio host who is known for her intellect, but not necessarily her intelligence about the natural world. He was explaining how the antelope graze peacefully with the lion in their midst, until that subtle moment when the cat widens her paws. This, too, is the reason the horse reacts with fear at the sight of the human hand, fingers outstretched. She interrupts to ask why the horse would mistake our hand for the dangerous claw of the predator. Roberts pauses, searching for a way to make the obvious politely clear. They make no mistake, he finally says. No mistake at all.

I have heard it said that becoming a parent is a lesson in self-lessness. The overwhelming urge to give and give again to your child is a way to find the hitherto unknown tap of generosity within. But even given the fact that most children are the result of a statement that begins "*I want* a baby," those first two words as far as I can tell the very definition of selfishness, the evidence given by my peers is more than a little contradictory. They seem to retreat inward from the world at large, because they have nothing left to give to it after giving so much to their children. They now work hard to provide for their families, but no longer for anyone else. The assertion about selflessness would be less disturbingly inexact were it not for the fact that a child is an avowed extension of oneself. Rather than recognizing that we give in to an utterly mindless instinct (not a slur, by the way, in my book), we take credit for deciding to create life; then we announce we are doing so selflessly, instead of giving to ourselves, or at least the little proxy composed of our biological material. We have a need to give; so we give ourselves the opportunity. Neither the baby nor the horse asked to be made.

I tell you nothing new. The world abounds with paradox, hypocrisy, denial, white lies. You knew that. Our primary mode of functioning may well be what the psychologists term projection, in which an uncomfortable truth is evicted and pinned onto the subject least able to resist, resulting in a fascinatingly precise reversal of truth: the deadly missile named Peacekeeper; hunters who want to be called conservationists; the rich saying the poor are greedy so as to pocket their pittances, too. *Populus vult decipi, ergo decipiatur:* the motto of our world. People want to be deceived, therefore let them be deceived. Nowhere are we more eager to be deceived than with our beloved, maligned, abused, exalted, misunderstood, miraculous horses.

Is this, then, the place to recall that the tenth and last avatar of Vishnu is Kalki, the horse that with a single blow of his hoof will explode the world?

10

BEGIN AGAIN

MY FIRST RIDING LESSON in more than twenty-five years was prefaced by an inadvertent scenic excursion lasting an hour and a half. The roads in this part of the country lack signs, for the most part, which would explain some of it; the rest was some garden-variety idiocy on the part of the driver. When at last I managed to find a telephone, which are in as short supply as road signs, I was crying in frustration. A thematic prelude to the act of taking up horseback riding again as an adult.

The advertisement that had led me down these circuitous roads read simply, "Learn to ride in harmony with the horse." Any more specificity would have been lost on me, who had last been instructed in "English"—meaning whatever saddle was around, on whatever horse was available. The only picture I possess of myself on a horse, from hundreds of hours spent thereon, shows me about to canter out of the frame, wearing bell-bottom jeans, hair flying, horse strung out and lacking any contact with the reins, and a smile of joy on my face; I was sitting on a saddle-seat saddle. I had also received jumping instruction at various points, sometimes with a forward-seat saddle and sometimes not. Needless to say, I do not know how to jump.

Luck and happenstance were about to deliver me to the place where I should have begun long ago, except that the world of riding had changed so much in the past quarter-century that the option barely existed for children then: dressage, a systematic method of learning to ride on flat ground that consists of getting one's body in enough control that one is able to get the horse's body in control. This is not the official definition, assuredly, which is closer to teaching the animal to do under saddle and weight what it does without teaching in nature.

The brand-new red barn and indoor arena has an interior that owes something to a Gothic cathedral, with sprung wooden arches soaring to the roof. This is appropriate given the reverence with which the training of horse and rider is pursued within its precincts. I am met by Dominique, a woman my own age, with bobbed black hair and a subtly chipped front tooth; her body is slender but looks like it contains tensile springs just under the skin. When she starts talking, she doesn't stop. She explains her methodology, and why what she teaches is about working *with* the horse and his biomechanical capabilities. When she next moves on to the subject of intelligence, how it is something that will expand if you expect it to, I feel a sudden jolt: Yes! This is something I had come to understand, quite by accident, in the process of training my Border collie, whose intelligence seemed to grow the more she learned and discovered she was capable of it. It had struck me, beautifully, magisterially almost, as a model of *all* animal intelligence, including human. I wanted to say, "Yes, yes, it's true—you know, I believe . . ." but there was no place for me to say anything. No doubt as it should be.

As I mounted Dandy, a thirteen-year-old Quarter Horse whom I later came to call Saint Dandy for his dignity and intellect and forbearance of riders far stupider than he, a familiar but long-absent feeling washed over me: the desire to please the teacher. The almost crippling desire to please the teacher. It had been lying in wait, where it wanted to reconnect me instantaneously to a childhood memory that I would have preferred to remain forgotten. Suddenly it was present, not as a thought or a recollection but as an inhabitant of my being, reshaping me from the interior like a Marvel comic-book character before I could even realize I should attempt to make it stop. It was the constancy of my semiconscious desire to hear the instructor say: "Wow, you have a *natural* talent for communicating with a horse." I had built entire castles in the sky on the foundation of this embarrassing wish as a child.

But the lesson of the lesson was to be the necessity of learning that there are no shortcuts, not with this horse business at any rate. It is plain hard work. I started to sweat under my borrowed hunt cap. I had walked in thinking I knew at least a little about riding; my knowledge lasted approximately six minutes. I was now down to zero. In subsequent lessons I would start mining a deficit. One solid bit of information that would stick conveyed the necessity, at this age, for wearing a sports bra to sit the trot.

Near the end of the lesson, Dominique called out to me, "Now, I want you to *think* about stopping." I had already figured out that my former wisdom concerning stopping, usually presented by my teachers as "Pull back on the reins," wasn't going to wash in this particular arena, not since notions of sense and weight and flow and breath and relaxation and lack of resistance had already been delivered as cornerstones of Dominique's methodology. So I did what she said. A voice inside my head whispered, "Stop," and that is all. Dandy took not one step more.

It was a miracle, and I reacted appropriately, sputtering and then sinking into bemusement. Dominique just smiled and nodded; the secret of this magic was old news to her. She went on to inform me that before the next lesson I would be well served by buying gloves, which would provide a more subtle feel of the reins, and proper breeches, which would help my seat. I knew it needed all the help it could get.

On the way home I kept replaying that moment when Dandy seemed to read my mind. If that was all it took to make a request, what, then, of all the horses whose mouths I had hauled on in the past? I had been taught to use a mace when a feather was the appropriate tool. And I had taught those horses—creatures that can feel you breathe, that can isolate the inch of skin on which a fly lands—that this is what life was like. The only protection they were to have was the power of the mind to dissociate from the body, and this they used until even a crop would draw forth only the detached look of someone who simply can't be bothered. Those were ghosts of horses. By now their bodies had been long dispatched to join their minds, wherever it is that worthy beasts go to find a freedom that lasts.

11

CODE

ADMIRE THE QUIET expertise of a woman who knows what she's doing around a horse; stand in the corner and watch. There is much to know. Bridles, bits, saddles, girths, pads, martingales, splint boots. She tacks up in a silence that seems compressed, punctured by a snapping-to of leather straps pulled through and secured. A sureness is expressed in the way the fingers go about their business, the way the eyes follow those fingers, a calm and certainty transferred to the horse. The two of them are nowhere but here, in no time but now. They are not even aware that they are being watched by someone else, with envious longing.

. . .

THIS IS A THEORY I contrived the day I was allowed to jump a one-foot rail but somehow managed to telegraph to my mount the news that we were about to enter the stadium at the Olympics and our team, nay, the entire country, was counting on us to have a fault-less round; he put an additional two and a half feet of air between his hooves and the wood, I lost my stirrups, and he put his head down with the intention of expressing an exuberant opinion of his rider's miscalculations. It is that riding is like windsurfing. When you first attempt it, you feel there's some alien force beneath you, utterly unpredictable. It surges like the water, and you fall the other way. You grab at something to get back onboard, flailing out. When you get better, and better, the wave underneath you starts to seem predictable, then part of you. Now you are riding it. And you have been trans-formed from the definition of ungainliness to the picture of poise.

IT IS A SENSUOUS business, and if you don't like touch, or beau-ty, you won't like this, the whole business of this. In the presence of grace embodied, one strives to be worthy.

> We tend to become passionately involved [with a pursuit] only when the ambiance appeals to our own romantic sense. Thus the attendant atmosphere to riding is, in my belief, not peripheral, but on the contrary, central to its passionate pur-suit. The accessories belonging to the equestrian atmos-phere, the beauty of a saddle, the feel of a glove, the elegance of boots, the glamour of an heirloom stock pin, all create enormous appeal, none less than the attentive eyes of our horse or his ears, his soft submission to our aiding system.

Or so says Charles De Kunffy in *The Ethics and Passions of Dressage*.

SOME GIRLS GO INTO ballet, others into riding; some try to do both, until their dance masters tell them it is time to choose: The muscles that must remain loose and limber for the plié and to enable the head to touch the straightened knee as the ankle rests on the barre are the same muscles that learn to cling tight to the saddle so that a sudden shy won't budge the seat. The turnout that is impressed on every ballerina's legs until she no longer recalls when she last walked with her toes pointing straight ahead would be a devil to the riding instructor, who would continually shout, "Toes in! You're looking like a duck."

But no matter which activity the young girl chooses, they are both ballet.

It is inevitable that wealth has come to be so closely associated with the form of dance that is equestrian activity, because wealth seeks out that which is rarefied, difficult to perfect, naturally conducive to subtle differentiations in levels of attainment. These will act as shelves on which to display—to whomsoever is educated enough to appreciate them—the trophies of arrival. The requirements of horse keeping keep becoming more difficult to fulfill as the twenty-first century arrives, all cluttered with houses, roads, developments, more and more stuff for more and more people and their cars. And so those who are able to provide for horses—animals whose basic needs refuse to advance from another era—show themselves above the exigencies of time and change. A bizarre sense of shock therefore accompanies the discovery that among the poor children of Dublin's public-housing ghettos, horses are popular pets.

Britain's royal family has long been the great avatar of what was once called "the horsey set." And the queen is an exemplary horsewoman, skilled and cool and obsessed in that distant way. Some have even complained, quietly and to themselves of course, that it appears she cares more, and is capable of feeling more emotion or at least some emotion, for her horses and corgis than for her subjects. Her daughter, Princess Anne, was steeped in the womb with this horsey love and came out so predisposed that her life has been devoted to riding with such single-minded purpose that she became an Olympic eventer.

America's royal family, the Kennedys, had Jacqueline Bouvier to give it the high sheen only an equestrian can give. At the time she was in school, riding was terribly elite; although her college had no on-campus riding program, there was a horse club, and the girls who belonged to it were wealthy and competitive, according to a woman who was there then, a horse lover who could not afford to keep a horse. Jackie was not a member of this club, but she did ride, "and she was a beautiful rider," which was corroborated for the viewer when she watched her compete in a show in which she took top honors. It is hard to imagine she would be otherwise. One of the most photographed women of her time, Jackie Kennedy Onassis remained most fond of one picture, that of herself on horseback.

One of New York's preeminent society designers has compiled a list of fourteen "essentials for a stylish life," and a horse makes company on it with "wonderful accessories" and "a good handbag."

If you want something to spend money on, you couldn't really do better than to get into horses, and to get into them competitively. Then you can spend upward of one hundred thousand dollars for a respectable show jumper, and dig a trench in which a steady stream of cash will run for board, training, grooming, shipping, lessons, entry fees, various furnishings, clothing, hotels, and air-conditioned trailers. Better yet, you could front a polo team, and in the space of one month, say, the one month surrounding the United States Polo Open, you could divest yourself of what is termed a cool million.

Or else you can be poor. You can be so good that rich people hire you to ride their horses. You can have a Bronx accent and still aspire to the Sport of Kings. You can be like at least one high school girl, who collects returnable soda cans to help finance her trip up through the ranks of competitive dressage, aiming for Grand Prix. You can own one snow-white saddle pad and work hard to keep it clean.

CLAREMONT RIDING ACADEMY, in the middle of Manhattan, is a place that turns the world feet-side up, so that you sense something is wrong but it takes a while to realize it, because no one seems to find it remarkable that everything is upside down. Horses live on the second floor, going up and down a spiral ramp covered with rubber matting and strips of wood placed every few feet for traction. They walk down into a room the size of a reasonable living room, and where the space would be dotted with sofas and tables there are instead metal columns from floor to ceiling. On weekends, as many as six lessons might be going on simultaneously, all manner of walk-trot-cantering, in the same direction. It looks like a life-scaled merry-go-round. But the horses are real, and after they are used, they go back up the ramp to be put away in the closet.

They live in the basement, too. I didn't know that until the second time I went there, when a voice called up from below: "Birchbark coming up!" and I looked to see a white and riderless horse, reins flapping against the hard-bobbing neck, coming up out of the dark all by himself. The groom at the bottom lets the horse go because there isn't room for the two of them side-by-side, and because the horse has to gather himself for an explosive plunge to get up the steep incline, and because where would he go, anyway, with the walls practically touching his sides? That's the thing about the whole place—where would he go, anyway? Claremont is all one big chute, essentially.

Nonetheless, it is an expensive chute, and its clientele are used to expensive things, and expensive things are generally what they want. Indeed, keeping a horse in Manhattan is the epitome of expansive wealth, and of the weird perversions that money can buy, as if money were of such little concern that you might consider installing a half-acre of grass lawn with a stream and a waterfall somewhere on East Fifty-eighth Street.

I go to meet a woman who keeps her beloved horse at Claremont; he is so beloved she cannot bear the thought of not seeing him every day. She seems shocked at the notion of having children: Why would I want children, when horses are so much better?

When she is finished riding, she dismounts and presses a button to open the electric garage door to the street and we walk the horse out to stand near the middle of Eighty-ninth Street. The cars go around us. It is Christmastime, so her tall black Thoroughbred gelding is wearing his maroon velvet dressage pad under his Passier saddle. Passersby in Central Park, she says, always call out in admiration of this perfect expression of seasonal cheer, and this is her goal: to envelop her horse in an aura of beauty that radiates out and catches everyone in its range. Then we reenter and go up the ramp into the ancient warren upstairs, the kind of strange dark place that leaves such a residue in my brain that it is bound to turn up in disturbingly sweaty dreams. She untacks and brushes and blankets her horse with a beautiful plaid blanket and suddenly some guy is there, opening a bag of new alfalfa-and-molasses feed—she wants only the best for him, and has spent much time searching out a wonderful holistic vet, the most delectable treats, healthy high-quality grain. She is investigating the possibility of having fresh alfalfa flown in from the West, because it is the finest in the land. She introduces the fellow who is rationing out the feed as her assistant—and for a moment I think, *Assistant for the horse? For her business? For her life?* I decided it was the latter, especially after he showed up a few moments later on the street to pick us up in a Range Rover that I took to be hers, which held her two Boston terriers and a box filled with many pots of blooming cyclamen. He asked politely if I would like him to pull over and get me some coffee or hot chocolate.

Instead I asked her what her horse would say to her if he could talk, and she asked him, "What in the world, dear, do you want most?" Without hesitation she answered in his voice, "A place to run and run, and to roll in the grass." They are so close she knows his mind well.

IT IS A SPORADICALLY gray summer day, humid, but relatively cool. I read over breakfast a newspaper item about where I am going to today, the Farmers' Museum Benefit Horse Show, which says everyone is encouraged to wear clothes that reflect the retro-

gressive nature of this "friendly competition": Straw hats are mentioned. The locale is Cooperstown, New York, an area that wears
its history on its sleeve; the air seems to change, to become dense
with good oxygen and subtle perfumes, as you drive north from
Oneonta, a wooden town in perpetual need of a paint job, toward
the village and its old stone buildings and ancient sheltering trees.

And so the scene of the show is suitably bucolic, the site the
former Iroquois Farm of one F. Ambrose Clark (1880–1964). He
"commenced development of this beautiful valley and hillside in
1901 when he was 22, by which time he was already world-
renowned for his skills in steeplechase riding and polo," according
to the program.

There are indeed a number of straw hats in the audience,
which numbers a couple of hundred. They wander slowly about
the grassy fields. The word *grosgrain* has for some reason formed
itself in my mind and will not leave.

There are so few competitors (which the young man doing
the announcing over the hesitant PA system never fails to call
"competititors") that the most any class has is four riders. Some,
including the final Adult Vintage Attire and Tack Stakes, have one;
blue ribbons are rarely so assured. (In this case it went to an
Appaloosa named Dakota, whose owner put an Indian blanket on
his back and a fringed Daniel Boone jacket and feather headdress
over her hunt attire.)

This is not a "rated" show, and the participants win nothing
more than ribbons and donated gifts of posters and saddle racks—
a few girls will amass a tack room's worth—but it is still a horse
show. It is still genteel, its own bubble-world of quiet manners and
adherence to a complex and historically engraved system of ethics.

I always have the feeling that when I venture onto show
grounds I am returning to a past that is alive still only within these
precincts. Not only is the world rarefied—a venue of high special-
ization where you may listen closely and recognize the language
as English but still not understand a word—but it is otherwise
gone. The laws that prevail here were formed in and informed by
a time that we passed on the road, oh, a long way back. Once these

rules were like all the other sets of rules, including what a lady did and did not do, dressing for dinner, the idea of honor. Now, that's a funny-sounding word, isn't it—*honor*. Personal honor. Honor toward one's country. Honor toward one's family, station, name. Whatever does it mean?

"Manners to be emphasized"; "appointments to count." I stand near the judges' tent and could hear them confer if only they were loudmouths, which they decidedly aren't. They are John and Elaine Moore Moffat, impeccable in their own appointments, and what you must call "true horsepeople." That is, by the way, a separate race. The Moffats, now apparently in their very well-preserved sixties, are credited with having run large shows in this area thirty years ago—big shows, real shows. He had been a trainer, she a qualifier for the United States Equestrian Team and author of *Earning Your Spurs*. Now she looks over the top of her reading glasses at her judging sheets and inclines her head toward him when he speaks but does not take her eyes off the ring (she is still pretty, blond, gold-earringed, and the kind of woman whom at one look you can see does not encourage argument). The only thing I hear her say, to her son, the ring steward, as she sends him off to disqualify a rider who has competed in a novice class even though she is beyond the specified novice age of twelve, is "You know, I'm sorry, but those are the rules, and the rules must be followed." It is not pissy, it is simply the way it is.

At the intermission there is an exhibition by the Otsego County 4-H Drill Team, which a few years back was named the New York State Champion Drill Team. All the riders are teenage girls. They look serious as all heck.

The music comes up over the tinny sound system; a light breeze threatens to carry off the sound. They move out. Their horses are all colors and sizes, and some require more vigorous encouragement with the legs and heels to work than others. The girls cast quick looks to one another to make certain they are in line in the serpentine, on time in the half-turn. At last they form themselves into a large pinwheel rotating through the entire space of the ring. The faces of the girls now are terribly intent, and I am standing captured within their compass. The inner horse is barely moving at all, turning on his forehand, while the outermost horse is being determinedly cantered by his rider. She urges him forward as if some unspeakable thing will happen to them both if he should lag and break the line that is almost straight even though each horse is progressing at a different speed. I watch their faces reveal the silent wishes each one fervently makes to her horse. My eyes have filled with tears.

THE RULES FOR A sidesaddle class at an American Horse Show Association show stipulate proper appointments: a sandwich case containing a hand-blown flask with sterling silver cap and cork liner, said flask to contain sherry or iced tea; a sandwich box of nickel-plated tin enclosing a sandwich of chicken, ham or tuna salad, or watercress. The crusts must be removed from the bread.

Well, of course the crusts must be removed.

At a large show such as the National at Madison Square Garden they still make an effort, too, serving champagne with a strawberry sunk in the admittedly plastic flute, even though it is hard to shake the knowledge that by sometime tomorrow night, just as three days ago, a shiny floor will send the sharp, echoing squeak of basketball shoes to the rafters, there to mingle with the smell of hot dogs. Things certainly change, as they say.

> The Horse Show, some two weeks earlier, had produced a passing semblance of reanimation [of post-summer New York society], filling the theatres and restaurants with a human display of the same costly and high-stepping kind as circled daily about its ring. In Miss Bart's world the Horse Show, and the public it attracted, had ostensibly to be classed among the spectacles disdained of the elect; but, as the feudal lord might sally forth to join in the dance on his village green, so society, unofficially and incidentally, still condescended to look in upon the scene.
>
> —*The House of Mirth* by Edith Wharton

Now, although viewers at even the most prestigious country shows may wear shorts and tennis shoes, walking around eating sandwiches with white liquid dripping out of them, the riders themselves emanate a dignity wholly of another time. Perhaps it is a testimony to the power of clothing, particularly clothing that has changed little in three hundred years. It is hard not to look elegant in trim breeches and custom-made boots. It is hard not to look like a member of an entirely different race of men when you wear them while lounging in a tent erected in the midst of a sea of green, sitting in a monogrammed director's chair set upon an Oriental rug over the ground and using a monogrammed tack trunk as a table for your crackers and cheese and gin and tonic while the glistening horses in the box stalls at your back move quietly to find a new spot in which to stand and rest.

Going into the Chelsea Equestrian Center, a chancy attempt to provide Manhattan riders with a cross between the university club and the top-of-the-line gym, my body starts to feel all the common symptoms of exposure to unrestricted sums of money: a mild, buried anxiety; evil curiosity; the twin pulls of jealousy and disgust, the stronger being jealousy. I am innocently talking to someone, hoping she doesn't hear the noisy calculating that is proceeding in my head: boots, $800, *ka-ching;* deerskin full-seat breeches, $250, *ka-ching;* British quilted barn jacket, $400, *ka-ching;* discreet gold and diamond earrings, $2,000, *ka-ching.* I can't stop myself. It is a sickness.

It is also nearly impossible not to think mean things as I watch from the viewing room above the arena that is supposed to house a coffee bar when it is finished and now contains the beginning of a "tack" shop that sells not tack, or much of it, but rather high-end equine kitsch, including exaggeratedly expensive silver and gold jewelry in the shape of hunt caps and bits.

A long-legged young man with a goatee bounces unmercifully on the back of a piebald whose ears tell what he thinks of the whole thing. A parade of horses with people on their backs circle, trot, canter, circle, as they are commanded. When they are finished, the horses are led to their stalls, brand-new but very much on the small side, where they will remain until the next time they are led out under saddle to circle the arena once more. They are allowed, two at a time, to be turned out in the outdoor ring, in the narrow space between the West Side Highway and the Hudson River. Periodically they are cycled out of the city to a place where they can get real turnout, to preclude their becoming sour. I see vinegar in some of their eyes right now.

What a bitter thing, too, I have become to look always underneath the furniture to see what dirt is left behind.

AND NO ACTIVITY pursued on horseback is as codified, stratified, and freighted with incendiary issues than foxhunting. Its rules on dress and behavior, from the ritual of the stirrup cup to jacket color to who may precede whom, make cutting off the crusts look like something every peasant does as a matter of course. In America it is yet another British import, like the Land Rover, that is employed as a semaphore for social (which in this country actually means financial) standing. Not to mention the fact that it is deliriously fun to ride a fine horse at a good clip over fences in the open countryside. The prime danger the sport is faced with on this side of the pond is the tendency of ignorant and nervous pop stars to buy estates in traditional hunt country and then close off the land to riders. That and the unimportant possibility that a few all-but-voiceless kooks will decry such a display of arrogant elitism as an affront to today's society that rivals staging a minstrel show or making one's housecleaner curtsy and back out of the room.

In Britain it is a different story, but a bit of the same. Only there is it conceivable that a bill to ban the hunting of mammals using dogs would be brought before Parliament (here the notion of cruelty to animals stands as much chance of being debated in Congress as whether to observe Lenin's birthday) and only there is it conceivable that such an act would bring one hundred thousand people to a rally against the bill. That is because a threat to foxhunting is seen as a threat to "a way of life." This might be translated as "the privileges of class," so long as you don't forget to factor in the sizable economy that grows up around any such activity. And also don't forget the fact that rituals comfort us as tight bunting comforts the newborn; we are perhaps conditioned from before birth to crave the small walls that tell us exactly where we are. Besides, no one likes to tear down historical buildings, even if they are beyond repair.

Tradition is supremely important to human culture, and it reacts as a serpent when threatened. It cannot be called wrong if it is what has been done for a long, long time. So the hunters everywhere are hanging on tight, as would anyone who has what they have. It is no surprise that they can field arguments to buttress every aspect of their right to continue doing what they have long done, and that these arguments wear the particularly steely armor that is standard issue to the legions of the status quo.

I was invited once to observe a hunt, and was therefore sent all the requisite information about the illustrious history of the hunt (even one that has existed for only a few years will have amassed an illustrious history), the Who's Who of the organization and their illustrious qualifications, the rules (the rules must be followed), and the options for participating as an outsider. One month later I received a sternly worded disinvitation from my would-be host. He had read something I had written about the sad life of the urban carriage horse, and had thereby discovered that my heart was not in the right place. I was a bad and dangerous sort of person, and moreover did not understand some very fundamental things about nature, which he sought to educate me about. I had called myself a lover of horses, and so did he. Only one of us was an impostor.

12

MESSIAH

WHEN MARY FIRST saw Jacob, the old ex-race-horse was 250 pounds underweight, and she was a forty-two-year-old beginner who had never before owned a horse. It was foolish beyond measure to buy an animal that could not be ridden, either then on a tryout or perhaps forever. But she couldn't leave him with an owner who could reduce an animal to such a deplorable state; her impulse to kindness was met with a price that was absurdly high, and that she paid with alacrity.

With much good feed and care, Mary restored Jacob. As justice sometimes does prevail, he turned out to be an ideal horse for a beginner, giving away nothing for free but displaying that quality that in horses is called honesty. She would ride him out on trails where they would both learn things. One day it was what would happen if they were set upon by two dogs. They snarled and barked and bit. Jacob stood there. He stood there as they tore his splint boots off and ripped at his knees with their teeth.

Nothing can convince Mary that Jacob did that for any other reason than to save her. Any other horse would have bolted in wild fear, become a manic streak of running. And as a beginner with an unsteady seat, she would have met the earth after a long arc through the air. So she vowed after that day to keep Jacob always, no matter what other horse she might get, no matter that he would before too long require her to give more to him than he was able to give to her.

She saved him, he saved her. You can't imagine how many times this story is told.

NATURALLY SUCH PERFECT reciprocity does not always materialize. Sometimes one is given to more than one gives. Then again, being the recipient of a great gift can prompt one to reflect on the nature of that gift, and so open up the mind and the heart and a channel for the backwash of compassion. There is always potential to redistribute wealth equitably.

Horses have taught me so much! I've learned to be more confident, more patient, more direct. Some people are able to articulate only this much of the vastness. But others are set off and running. One woman intends to write a book on how riding is analogous to living life, on how it presents the possibility of reawakening the dormant, essential self. She repeats the refrain of women who as girls loved horses and never "gave it up"—without knowing why, they kept their hats and their saddles, dragging them from city apartment to city apartment; they kept their hope in the spirit form of these vestiges. And as if making a sacred vow (a vow, really, of marriage: to unite two broken-away parts of self—child and whatever passes for the rest), they promise themselves to get a horse again someday.

Another talks of the *way* you ride as amounting to nothing short of an entire philosophy of living. This belief seems to come up, interestingly enough, only with those who have ultimately found their way, sometimes along a winding trail past all manner of grotesque or indifferent methodologies, to disciplines such as dressage, Centered Riding, natural horsemanship, and their ilk. (Philosophical they are, too. One woman points out that the hunt seat is "goal-oriented," looking always ahead to the next moment in the form of the next fence, the opposite of the Zen-like centered seat, in which you seek to be in the moment, as closely connected to the horse as it is possible to be.) They are ways of relating that depend upon, and in fact cannot be truly accomplished without, the following: absolute free flow; the removal of internal and external impediments to both mind and body; honest and sure communication; and complete trust in the horse's ability to reverse the flow of information back to you so long as you listen with an open, reflexive mind. The voice on the other end of the phone tells me, with directness and clarity, that the way she has learned to communicate with horses—with directness and clarity—often sets her apart from others. "People who are not horsepeople are simply unable to understand a very important part of me. They do not know that I mean what I say—that my demands are unequivocal, that I don't fuck around. I mean what I say because that is the way you talk to a horse, the way you *must* talk to a horse." She and her kind speak of riding as a path to illumination, the way to attaining a moment of limpidity: leaving confusion behind. (As much as to say; leaving most of life behind.) You simply can't be confused on a horse, or it all goes to shit. Amazingly fast. "They can hear you breathing. They know your mind."

WATCH THIS DEMONSTRATION of therapeutic riding. On the showgrounds, a doctor with a microphone is describing how hippotherapy is a prescription he will write down on a pad, just like an antibiotic. Unlike an antibiotic, it can be good for so many ills, they still haven't cataloged them all yet: autism, cerebral palsy, juvenile delinquency, drug addiction, afflictions of heart and body both. The horses here have just come off the jumping course; this is a first for them. The two little girls have cerebral palsy; they cannot walk. Each joins together with a horse to form one being. The human borrows the horse's locomotion, and for the first time her body experiences the sensation of moving on its own, the spine undulating, the muscles and bones rocking and rippling. (The wheelchair may move her from place to place, but in it she herself remains motionless; only the horse allows her to get this feeling into her bones so that they may come to remember it, perhaps to replicate it.) As they go around the ring, tiny packages of flawed flesh perched atop massive beings of perfect form, the doctor is saying how horses are such excellent therapists that if they could become doctors, he'd be out of business. You can tell from the way he says it that this is not meant as a joke. The literature is in fact filled with anecdotes amounting to as much proof as you could want: the child who for years has not spoken and up there on top of a horse says her first word; the boy whose neuromotor damage causes him to twitch almost continually becomes calm and stately on the back of the horse. Miracles and more miracles, the parents say. The horses are silent, going about their work. Everyone agrees, though, that they, too, are somewhat transformed: They instantly, intimately, identify their cargo through means known only by them. Take even the ornery mount; watch him become gentle and slow, but only for the damaged ones. He will still kick you, strong predator, in the teeth. They can hear you breathing, and they know your mind.

THEY WILL SAVE YOU. This is a story from a magazine, and it must be true. The grade mare gets a new partner, a big black gelding of unknown provenance. They coexist peacefully in the pasture until one day. That is the day the mother watches from the window to see her three-year-old daughter wandering into the pasture to say hello to her friend the mare. The gelding watches her from the other end of the field. Then he decides to act. He whirls. At a gallop, ears back, teeth bared, he runs straight for the child. So, too, does the mare run, once she sees the big black coming. She reaches the girl just in time to interpose herself and receive his blow. Then she turns her backside to him and pummels him into retreat. The mother does not hesitate to describe the mare's next act as going over to the child "to see if she was all right." The animal behaviorist is not so sure about this; it is dangerous to impute human motivations to a horse, who likely has entirely something else in mind. It is equally dangerous to imagine you have not seen what you have certainly seen.

DO YOU THINK I mean to say that only women love horses? Those who love them enough to try to save them, and be saved by them, are not restricted by gender, but only by the state of their souls. It was a man, Robert Bontine Cunninghame-Graham, who famously said, "God forbid that I should go to any heaven in which there are no horses." Along similar lines but about twenty years before, in 1888, John Codman wrote in *Winter Sketches from the Saddle,* "I believe the horse has a soul. The Bible tells us that there are horses in heaven, and that they came down from thence to take up Elijah. I think that even bad men get to heaven at last, and there is no reason why horses, who are better than they are, should not get there before them." This is also the author who espouses the physically and emotionally salutary benefits of what he terms Equestrianopathy and who directs every horseman to "hang about the stable until your horse is fed. Get your own dinner afterwards for you are of less importance." A sentiment no doubt shared by Albion Winegar Tourgée, a popular novelist of the Reconstruction era of whom Edmund Wilson noted in *Patriotic Gore:* "he once started a novel called *My Horses,* and the horses in his other novels are personalities as important as their owners." Another whose fellow feeling for horses sets him apart not only from his gender but from his species in general was the Russian poet Vladimir Mayakovsky; his 1918 poem "Concern for Horses" speaks quite eloquently for itself. It also intimates what just may be the ultimate source for all such preternatural identification with the powerless and oppressed no matter what species (and here I must tread light-ly, for I venture into that dangerously unpopular territory marked "psychology") simply through its voice, which, as described by the poet's translator, Maria Enzensberger, is "anguished, suffering from profound loneliness and a lack of understanding and compassion."

> *Hoofs sang*
> *stamping the ground:*
> *'Grot,*
> *Grand,*
> *Grit,*
> *Groomed.'*
> *Ice-shod,*
> *wind-hounded,*
> *the street*
> *skidded underfoot.*
> *Suddenly,*
> *a horse slumped on its croup.*
> *At once,*
> *all those drifters flared-trousered*
> *gathered in force.*
> *Laughter*
> *spilled and spouted:*
> *'A horse tumbled!*
> *Look at the horse!'*
> *The Kuznétsky rumbled.*
> *Only I*
> *didn't join my voice in the sneering.*
> *I came nearer*
>   *and saw*
> *the eye of the horse . . .*
> *The street, tipped over,*
> *continued on its course . . .*
> *I came nearer*
>   *and saw*

a large tear
　　　roll down the muzzle,
glisten,
　　　and disappear . . .
And some sort of fellow animal pain
splashed out of me
and flowed in whispering:
'Horse, please . . .
Horse, listen,
why should you think you are any worse?
Darling,
we are all
　　　essentially horses,
each and every one of us is something of a horse.'
Maybe
　　　the old one
　　　　　didn't need my comfort,
maybe
　　my thought
　　　　　was too effete,
only the horse tried hard,
　　　　　neighed loud,
rose to its feet,
　　　and made a start.
Its tail playing
　　　in glittering coat,
it trotted indomitably toward its stall,
It suddenly felt
　　　it was still a colt
and life was definitely worth living again.

"There are no differences between men and women in the emotions they feel or in how intensely they feel them. The differences in expression we see today emerged because women are expected, allowed, and required to reveal certain emotions, and men are expected and required to deny or suppress them. These rules of emotion are not arbitrary; they fit our social arrangements. It wasn't always so." We are always trying to figure out who we are and why, and we are finding that it is a complicated business indeed, and that we will probably never know who we are and why—all those forces at work, inside us and outside, all the mass of the unspoken and unregistered. That opinion above comes from Carol Tavris in *The Mismeasure of Woman;* she believes that when the industrial revolution polarized work and home and conse-quently the sexes, the roles we seem to accept as normal—woman as nurturer, man as aggressor—were created. Other writers have recently posited a golden age when matriarchal societies empha-sized rule based on partnership and creativity, as opposed to dom-ination and destruction (humbug, say the scholars); specialists in communication behavior have found that women, at least now, consistently attempt to forge alliances and smooth exchanges with others, while men tend toward a canine model of establishing hierarchy. When it comes to horses, the questers after knowledge will find that what is old is new, and news.

You can break a horse. You can humble him with violence and shackle him until he submits. You can meet "disobedience" with a quick whip; that's what some people do to their children, and it works, too, until the child grows up, but by then he's someone else's problem. Or you can honor his nature. You can demand not that he learn your language but that you learn his. Understanding, even the will to understand, can look like magic. It is the latest thing: the western style of working with who the horse is, rather than who you impatiently wish him to become. People the world over line up for miles for tickets to fill the stadia at stops on the natural horsemanship roadshow. This is not a new technique, however, this horse whispering. It is not even an old secret of the cowboys, just coming to light once more. It is the way it has always been done by the thoughtful, the intelligent, the ones with unruined hearts. Even for the solely pragmatic, it is the way it works best:

> Should any of my readers think that these views of the relations between horse and rider are too sentimental, that

all which is needed in a horse is easy movement, obedience to the reins, and readiness to go forward when urged,
and that love and respect are quite unnecessary, she will
find, should she ever meet with any really alarming object
on the road, that a little of this despised affection and confidence is very desirable, for, in the moment of danger, the
voice which has never spoken in caressing accents, nor
sought to win confidence will be unheeded: fear will prevail over careful training, and the rider will be very fortu-
nate if she escapes without an accident.

That is the soft but commanding voice of Elizabeth Karr again,
calling out from 1884. Her natural wisdom is kindred blood with
what has been known by generations of farmers who yoked to the
plow the massive draft horse, the animal that is cold-blooded, yes,
but that still and forever retains an imprint of the swift-to-react
prey. So, encourages the *Work Horse Handbook,* "Work to develop
the horse as your teammate. Think about the horse as your equivalent and see and feel his limitations as your own."

Empathy; what an idea. *Think about the horse as your equivalent.*
Not only could it make you millions if you publish a best-selling
book about it, it could single-handedly halt misery on its
Sherman's march through the ranks of all poor beasts of burden.
But empathy is not an idea that sells well to the bulk of humani-
ty, particularly if it is directed toward nonhumans. Have no fear:
The patent on your specialty will not be challenged by too many.

IN 1919, THE PALESTINE campaign ended, the twenty thousand remaining horses of the victorious British were sold to the
Egyptians. Having been in Egypt, and thus knowing exactly what
it would mean, some of the Yeomen shot their mounts rather than
allow them to face what that particular future held for them.

Eleven years later, Dorothy Brooke, the wife of the cavalry
commander in Egypt, was overcome by a wave of sympathy. She
set about locating whatever British horses might have survived

their ordeal. Amazingly, she found several hundred—several hundred starved, beaten, dejected, barely alive horses. She wrote to *The Morning Post* in London, asking for help in securing funds to buy them out of their slavery. Ultimately, forty thousand pounds was donated to the Old War Horse Fund, and she established a hospital (now the renowned Brooke Hospital for Animals, in Cairo). She also got the government to assure that they would never again commit the shameful act of selling their war horses to foreigners. Of course, this happened in 1935, when horses were at last about to be relieved from their millennia as conscripted cannon fodder. But she had done what she could.

Doing what they can is all any of them are able to do, the small-time saviors in a desert of death. Fewer than 1 percent of horses in this horse-mad land get to retire to a field to eat grass until they die; the rest are trailered off to the potter's field of a pet-food can or a dinner plate in Europe, or are left to die of starvation and other results of human stupidity, or become test subjects until the tests do them in, or are recast as the raw material from which the drugs that will keep us happy, never mind them, are produced.

If you don't believe in luck, then you have never visited Mylestone Equine Rescue, Colorado Horse Rescue, the Hooved Animal Humane Society, Equus Sanctuary, Ada Cole Rescue Stables, Redwings Horse Sanctuary. There you will find the very emblems of luck, the horses who were still standing when the emergency van arrived, the horses who drew in the form of a long straw a judge who agreed to the impoundment, the horses who happened to live in a county with an active humane society instead of one where it is left up to the police, who have no idea what they're seeing when they see a horse that is tottering near the line beyond which there is no hope. They tell amazing stories, these lucky ones, though to call them lucky sticks in the throat after you hear how they came to be here: the horse whose blanket was not taken off for months, so the man who was supposed to be feeding him "didn't know" he was getting so thin; the horses who had been captive in uncleaned stalls for years, so they stood, heads bowed near the ceiling, atop four feet of manure; the pony left tied in the shed to eat the wood of his cell, and his untrimmed hooves curling up to his shins like elf boots, but elf boots that have permanently crippled him; the herd turned out in a paddock of dust along with the bloated corpses of several mates who had led the way to where they were soon to go; the ex–show horse whose tendons had given way at a young age and whose journey to the slaughterhouse was waylaid at the last minute by one bid that just exceeded the most the killer buyers were willing to pay. For every one of these there are hundreds of others who went unfound, unseen, unheard, unsaved.

The founder of one equine welfare group reminds me that despair is a sin. She says she doesn't care anymore what people think of her, whether they like her or think she is a moral misfit to care for animals, to work so many years on their behalf. She says she thinks only of the animals.

She tells me there are three types of women who love horses: those who want something out of them, personally or profession-ally; those who anthropomorphize them; and those who are seeking a higher knowledge about horses and humans and the mysteries of their intersection. She does not need to say which is in her opinion by far the smallest group. In her office she opens the mail: a package of color five-by-seven scenes from an equine slaughterhouse, and even she who has been in one looks at a few, then sets the rest on the desk, facedown. But someone else has been brave enough to take them, and it is a good thing, because pictures are the only thing that can stand up, if anything can, and because the media, in their insatiable lust for gore, want them. She takes a call on her cell phone about some neglected horses in a nearby field, telling the ignorant girl on the other end, "Don't give them any more apples—you could kill them. In their state they should get only grass hay. *Grass* hay, not any other kind, okay? Can you get some bales and throw them in?" She rolls her eyes when she gets off. She has no more patience left, not only for this girl but for anyone, anywhere. She seems to have given it all away years ago, and has no desire to replenish the store. It is a patience-sapping business, caring so much that you hurt all the time, that you can't sleep for the blood and flesh hanging in tatters and screams of pain and dead eyes that stare at you in dreams. This is what happens once you look at the pictures; it is what happens once you know what really happens.

I HAVE GONE TO visit someone I haven't met before. It is winter, and the landscape is gray and the ground dull and muddy; it makes me feel vaguely depressed.

Ramona is an artist of some sort, though I never find out what kind of work she does. Instead, the eighty acres of slightly rolling field and woods, thickly settled around with houses in another sign that the countryside is no match for the suburbs, are dotted with huge abstract sculptures put there by her companion, Sid, a former art dealer. Both of them have left New York behind for the comfort of animals and mud and growing things.

There is something very girlish about Ramona, although her short straight hair is peppered with gray. She speaks with a southern accent so faint it is an ancient perfume. She wears riding tights, cozy-looking leggings with straps under the feet. She had not, however, been riding that day, the ground cold and covered with slush.

We spend a great deal of time in the house, just a little unkempt and chilly. Everywhere are beautiful photographs of the horses in impressive frames: Clara, a light gray Thoroughbred, and Ghost, her three-year-old son, sired by a Dutch warmblood. Over a lunch of miso soup I hear many stories of the amazing exploits of these two.

Ramona speaks often of instances when one or another of the horses become "blocked" or "just not present," as when they would advance up the unfenced hill and then not seem to hear their names being called. Or if they stumbled or fell ill, they would be said to have "gone away." Ramona says this with an ineffably sad look, as if she were saying they had died. Or she says their energy was blocked; she practices acupressure, and says she allows the "energy" of the patient (whether equine or human) to "move" her hands for her, which do not even have to touch the skin to be effective. (She later demonstrates this on Ghost's haunch, and when she lets her fingers descend to his skin to touch what she calls the pressure points, he kicks out at her and then moves away. This to her is definitive proof that letting the energy direct the hands, as opposed to being guided by impersonal authority, is superior, although it might look to anyone else that she had merely touched a sensitive spot too hard. Likewise, Ghost's left eyelid is at half-mast, and a well-worn tear path descends from the eye, but Ramona says with certainty, "Nothing is wrong with his eye. It's just that way.")

She clears away the dishes and lets me read a remarkable magazine article she has saved from an old issue of *Practical Horseman* on nonviolent horse breaking, a step-by-step pictorial showing a lean blond trainer using her body—but no contact whatsoever—to communicate with the horse. The movements are extremely subtle (a directional hip thrust or several steps taken backward while sliding one leg behind the other and bending the knees, an apparent combination of Balinese dancing and Tai Chi) to make the horse move this way or that, stop or turn or face away. The power she exerts over her subject is that of a marionetteer, or, more properly, a magical one who does not even require strings. It reminds me of the plastic ballerina I had as a child, which spun on a mirror when a magnet was brought near. I might also have been reminded of the "natural horsemanship" methods of getting a horse to latch on or "Join Up," if my viewing of this article had not preceded their reintroduction on a popular scale by several years.

But more amazing than this are the sensuous black-and-white photographs she pulls out next, of the artwork her animals have produced. The hens and the pheasants laid eggs among straw and shredded newspaper that clung to their surface to make suggestive collages. And the horses had been given an easel and cray-pas of their very own! (Ramona says it was because they had "asked" her, and she quoted them, for "some of those cray-pas like you used to have when you were a child.") They hold a pastel or charcoal stick between their teeth, Ramona explains, via a rubber holder like that on a pot handle. She holds up a sketchbook, and the resulting drawings, very much like children's early work, are, at the least, wonderfully open to interpretation. The horses' greatest work, however, was performed upon each other, in the form of mutual mane braiding. In another age, Ramona would have been producing the evidence by which she would have been condemned to burn at the stake, since it was a sure sign of witchcraft to provoke horses' manes to braid themselves spontaneously. But now it was considered horses' mystery, not humans', that they toyed with their lips upon the manes of others and sometimes the results were magnificent: The pony (recently deceased) bore a long, multicolored twirl in the middle of his flowing mane; other examples were nearly perfect braids, as symmetrical as any produced by human hands, while yet others formed elaborate Celtic knots, as if just a few strands of mane or tail had been deliberately—and agilely—interwoven for ornament (and they had stayed, Ramona asserted, better than the braids of a professional she had paid to do Clara's mane for her first appearance in the dressage ring).

It is near twilight when we finally go outside to see the horses in the flesh. Ramona made a little shrine of a room in their two-stall barn in which she had set the mail, cards and letters addressed to the horses, and a rubber vase filled with now-dead flowers—"Clara likes irises especially"—which makes me want to go outside again, into the solace of the gray and mud.

But outside makes me want to go in, since outside the two horses are confined for the evening in a small pen. Clara, light gray and friendly, paces a well-worn circle and cribs always in the same two spots. Ghost, handsome and wild, being a young stallion, tosses his head and darts about in the mud, occasionally allowing a pet or two, but always craning around to try to get a bite of jacket or arm. But my eye is drawn to the next pen, where Zane, a woolly Quarter Horse, is tied to his lean-to. He looks dejected as only a tied horse can. So, although he is not as beautiful or favored as mother and son, or probably because he is not, I am drawn to him.

Ramona reveals the reasons for his status: first day of hunting season; the nonfunctionality of the electrified cord around his paddock; his natural propensity for escape. The risk simply cannot be taken, especially since you don't have to look far for stories of how family pets, goats, horses, and even cows are routinely taken down by a hunter eager to shoot, anything. The situation is even more vivid to Ramona, who the year before had been outside grooming the yearling Ghost when she looked up to see a hunter on the property next to hers looking through the scope of his rifle right between the young horse's eyes—and thus Ramona's as well, as her head was directly behind his.

So when Ramona says that before dinner she always lets the horses out to graze and gambol on the open hill where Sid had placed the monumental abstract sculpture he collected, I ask if I could let Zane out, too, to hand-graze on a lead.

I feel very much as I do when I let my two dogs run in the park, where they are free to go as far and fast as they want; I must merely trust that they will come back as they always have. Their happiness and freedom are the price of my anxiety. Usually they growl and snap and bodycheck and mock fight as they go.

Ghost now wants to do the same thing, and he suddenly rushes up to Zane, nostrils flaring, then wheels and presents his backside as if in preparation for a kick. All well and good—horses, like dogs, know much better than humans how to deal with their own behavior. Except for one thing: I am on one end of the rope attached to one of these horses, and if I let it go, that horse would then be free to go. And go. I have only my voice to discourage the thousand pounds of Ghost's determination to get a rise out of the gelding, and it works as half-assedly as you might imagine.

Every time Zane decides to move to better grass, it provokes a storm in Ghost. He rears and races toward us, and Zane wants to assert his own desires in the matter. But he never does.

Just before I leave, Ramona tells me Zane had been protecting me, that he knew what the consequences for me would have been had he rassled with his mate. She had watched us from the barn. And when she comes back from delivering his night's hay and before she turns on the CD of the chamber music she plays every night before the horses' bedtime on the player she has bought just for them, she informs me that Zane had told her to tell me that I was welcome to come back and ride him. It would be, he said, his pleasure.

13

PERSONALS

YESTERDAY I MOVED a ton of manure. Actually, it was the horses who moved it; I merely pitched it into a wheelbarrow and rumbled it over the rocky dirt and up to the top of the pile of more manure, then upended it and began again—a true Sisyphean task, because the cart always rolls back down, and you always have to go up once more. It gave me new appreciation for the digestive systems of these animals, with their constant need for grass or grass substitutes to be moving through the colon.

I have become one of the small army of part-time workers at Dominique's barn offsetting the cost of lessons by doing the endless things that need doing. And, indeed, she runs her establishment with martial precision, though there is never the sense that these are the kind of orders one chafes under, the kind meant to bat you into line. You just do them, because you are getting something better than money in return: the opportunity to take her orders in the ring.

We are, in fact, a small army composed of slave masters who are in turn enslaved by our slaves. We are the ones who assiduously pick up their excrement behind them, the ones who put our hands under their penile sheaths on a regular basis to make sure they're clean. We bathe, curry, brush, mane-pull, tail-detangle, hoof-pick, daub with salve, apply spray, and take off and put on blankets, fly sheets, leg wraps, bell boots. They stand there and loudly demand their food.

Yet, go into a stall; close the door. Wait a moment. Something will occur to you, something that seems to shift in the air between the two of you. It is the weight of power, the weightlessness of vulnerability, exchanging ions. The horse is there looking at you with eyes the color of chocolate pudding. He cannot escape you, or whatever it is you mean to do with him.

THIS PARTICULAR ARMY is rather haphazard in organization, yet everything gets done: I have never been in a stable so clean. *Standards*—the highest of them. Aisles swept, stalls picked out several times a day, water buckets scrubbed and refilled. Brushes cleaned, tack soaped. No aesthetic overlay, however: no flowers by the driveway or sign to announce the place's name, a couch barely fit for the Salvation Army in the viewing room, and, more often than not, no paper towels in the bathroom. But the working bolts, in their well-oiled condition, are their own visual pleasure. The horses, the order, the order.

The first of the two sergeants in the line of command is Amelia, barn manager. A flow of wavy light brown hair, pleasant steady demeanor, quiet. She has, Dominique says, one of the great posts—elegant, natural. This is no doubt aided by her body, which

is trim and athletic and without any folderol at all. She does everything as Dominique decrees, often as she pauses in the middle of
the arena while seated atop her horse: "Amelia, please give Deedee
an extra flake of hay, then bring in Jesse from outside. When you're
finished with that, get Dandy ready for the lesson. You can use the
Wintec. Oh, and since we don't have any clean pads, look through
the pile to find the best—I think Wilant's will be okay; he didn't
exactly sweat today." Stuart, the second sergeant, is a friendly ex-
city refugee with buzz-cut red hair, a former teacher of guitar. He
likes to have music on as he works, Lou Reed or occasionally
Classical Music's Great Waltzes. On it goes: "Stuart, you can do the
buckets on this side, and then a quick pick run on the other."
Along with the stacking of hay and shoveling of sawdust, Stuart
builds and fixes everything from new paddocks to tack boxes to a
hayloft and additional stalls.

Then there is Catherine, Dominique's protégée. She's like any
pretty teenager with porcelain skin and fine lemon-colored hair;
her cheeks flush deep rose as she spends hours picking rocks out
of the paddocks under a hot summer sun at Dominique's request,
but it seems she doesn't sweat. She has one of those purely
American, corn-fed, "large-boned" frames, completely in accord
with that of her seventeen-hand horse, Fury, whom she rides in
dressage competition. She wants to go as far as she can, she says, to
Grand Prix if possible, "though most people don't know just how
much work this is." She has the legs to be able to communicate
with the big ("Yeah, a big teddy bear!") animal. Another fre-
quenter of the barn comments with a laugh how butch she looks
when riding with two whips: "Pop-pop-pop! Man, I love it!"
Catherine and Dominique are more like school pals than teacher
and student separated by more than twenty years; they crack up
uncontrollably when one of them says, "People hear the name
Fury and expect this great wild thing—ha ha ha!"

Besides Stuart and one other fellow who has come in for a les-
son or two, everyone who works there or learns there is female.
(Dominique jokes that she is going to rename the place Tits-in-
Front Farm, since that is the posture correction she makes most

constantly.) That is, until Dominique advertises in *The Chronicle of the Horse* for a full-time working student and gets Frank.

I talk with him as I stand in the tack room oiling Dominique's double bridle, so new it is stiff and the black dye comes off with the saddle soap. I ask him where he comes from; I am curious ever since two days ago, when I first saw him momentarily doff his ever-present cap to reveal his balding head and suddenly appear much older than I thought he was. His lanky body, perfect for the old-fashioned thigh-balloon breeches he favors, makes him look exactly like one of those young British cavalry officers of the twenties or thirties who used themselves to illustrate their own riding manuals. Now I realize: *Not just starting out—starting over.*

He has previously worked with Standardbreds, raising and training harness racers. Now, he says, the stakes are getting too rich for his blood, with good yearlings going for fifty thousand dollars and Canadians and even Europeans getting involved more and more. He moved to another stable nearby, but some family intrigue or other—he was very vague—made him want to leave.

He says he is here now, beginning a new thing entirely, because he is motivated to become a better horseman. Because all of the good horsemen he knows are good people, too. There is a correlation at the deepest level, he says: compassion for the animal, desire to do right, the need for "clean living." I sense he is not referring to lots of carrot juice and regular visits to the gym; this is the old construct, and I smell religion lurking nearby, just as I feel sadness coming off him even when he means to reveal nothing.

I WATCH DOMINIQUE as I do my work, and I get good at not gawking too obviously. She reminds me of a dog trainer I knew, a trainer whom people accused of committing miracles. There is that look of tight focus, the tendency to teach by praise, and to come down on a fault "like a bolt of lightning," in the trainer's words, and just as quickly to release the pressure. When a couple of horses in the box stalls that line the two aisles are participating in some foolishness together—"They want attention," she says, "but I'm going to show them that's not the way to get it"—her body suddenly compresses, losing a fifth of its size. She moves so fast it's as if she's done a sci-fi teleportation, suddenly disappearing from the arena only to reappear near the tack room, where she picks up a dressage whip. In another flash she's in Wilant's stall. "Do you see this whip? Do you see that wall? I am hitting that wall"—*whap, whap, whap*—"so you know never, never to do that. And you, too"—now she's in the next stall—"don't play around with"—*whap*—"that crap. I've had it." She closes the door and walks away. The horses have not been frightened, exactly; they look like students who have been caught out. A few minutes later she looks back at Wilant, who now bears a different look, and she interprets it in cartoon-character words: "'What'd *I* do? *I* didn't do nothin'!'" She laughs.

Then she is schooling a student's horse, and she talks incessantly. "*Good* boy, *good* boy—whoops, not that—I said *not* that—you're not going to do that—*good* boy—yes, yes." Of course, her body is doing the real talking. She is keeping him "round," "soft," "moving out," "gathered up," keeping him from swinging his hindquarters around as they circle, and especially from dropping his head and shoulder down as they circle to the right. Later she explains, "His head is, what—two hundred pounds? I'm not going to *carry* it for him." They canter in tiny circles, and the pace never varies.

IT ENLIVENS MY TIME, not to mention me, to have a special horse to love. But it would be too heartbreaking, like choosing another woman's man, to settle on one of the boarders' horses; instead I choose, or am chosen by, Wilant, one of the two school horses. He is a large Dutch warmblood with a black mane and tail; a wash of dapples over his body is so light that it requires the sun to become visible. One of his eyelids droops away from his eyeball at the bottom, as if it had gotten hooked on something once.

Actually, I have fallen for him slowly, during which time he gradually became "my boy." There is something adolescent and unprotected about him. Dominique says he came from a rider who did not know how to ride him—she was not malicious, but her inabilities allowed twists and constrictions to cramp him into unhappiness. It has taken Dominique time to free him again, to show him how to flex and stretch and cure himself. He will never, though, stop hanging his great pink tongue out the side of his mouth as he works, or become angry enough for fits of head-tossing if a rider has heavy hands. While I am on his back I try to will my weight away from him so as not to hurt him; his head remains perfectly still with me because I attempt no contact at all—a petty form of abuse, Dominique informs me, since it leaves a horse directionless. But she is amused by the deal we seem to have struck: I won't ask him to work very hard, and he won't put up a fuss with me.

So it is a real surprise one weekend when Monica, the wealthy girlfriend of the man who financed the barn and known by some as the Contessa—she of the Cinderella's sister demeanor, perennially cross and critical—while showing me how to polo wrap Wil's legs (condescendingly: "Now, if you expect to do dressage, you have to learn to polo wrap"), stops and rests her hand on his rump. Her eyes squeeze into a terse black line. "If you ride him badly, I'll *kill* you."

Later Frank is working in Wil's stall as I slip in to give him a good-bye carrot; I have become a walking cliché. "You know, I have to tell you," I say, "I've sort of fallen for Wil."

"What is it about Wil?" he asks. "Everyone here's in love with him—you, Dominique, Monica."

"It's that combination of 'Please be kind, please' with this big hunk of manliness," I explain. "You know, the paradox of *Take care of me—I can take care of myself*?"

"No," Frank says.

I WATCH UNSEEN from across the barn as Amelia, untacking Lupe, plants a little kiss on his withers minutes after he has bucked

his way around the ring with her onboard. He is a particularly difficult case, coming from the racetrack, where the grooms liked to
play a little "game" with him, turning him into a cantankerous
biter. But any horse's misbehavior or difficulty seems to make
Amelia soften all the more, and the louder they get, the calmer she
gets. She is constantly talking to and smoothing them, even when
she is talking to someone else, unlike so many riders who seem
barely to notice there's a breathing thing on the other end of the
lead they're hauling on. She is becoming my model for how to be
with horses, for nothing they do seems to inspire either anger or
fear in her. The next horse she rides, Chocolate, has decided no
one should mount him unaided from the ground, and when she
tries he succeeds in tipping her over onto her rear and then runs
around the ring loose. She springs up and runs toward him, wav-
ing her arms, to spook him away from the open door. Then she
asks for a leg up and mounts him. She speaks in low tones to him,
and he soon lowers his head in relaxation.

FRANK DOESN'T LAST long; perhaps his desire for clean living
is not being met here, or perhaps he does not believe that horses
are as Dominique says they are, as she acts they are with every
move in her repertoire. The next working student, and the ones
after her, will be young women.

Likewise, Wilant does not remain alone in my affections, not
after the arrival of Dutchess, a draft cross with the coloring of a
cow and a head about the same size. I start loving her the moment
Dominique comments that we look good together as we go
around the ring—this is yet another shameful thing that speaks
unkindly of my character—and I continue loving her as I build
fantasies that maybe she, finally, after all these years, would be my
first horse, responding to the propitious omen of my having
bought a house located between those of two women who own
horses. Only there is no one who will give me the twenty-five
hundred dollars she will cost as well as the indeterminate amount
more it would take to keep her.

She is strangely aloof, taking carrots but never presuming thereafter that they are her due. I have always been attracted to the thick exterior, and I set about trying to see if in her case it conceals a wounded softness within. I think we look for mirrors in our love. One night I dream that she has reared up to put her front legs around my shoulders in a hug, but when I wake I realize I must have conflated her with my black-and-white girl dog, who can actually do that without killing me in order to express her regard.

I sit on the floor of her stall, writing. I note that if the pen slips, it is because she is looking for, though not demanding, more carrots. Her head is down in my lap—a *big* head. Her lips are pink, wrinkled, and hairless, human skin, baby skin. I pay no attention to the music Stuart is playing—his taste describes everything mine is not, and sometimes Catherine and I exchange a glance when he leaves the barn and move as one to change the tape—but suddenly I become aware of the words Rod Stewart is singing at that moment: "You're in my heart, you're in my soul . . ." I laugh, because you couldn't put something like that in a movie; stupidly, ludicrously, obvious. Her ears are large and bovine, and her lips and tongue, though so large as well, are delicate enough to take a fingernail-size piece of the dried mango I am eating. She stands quietly over me right now, larger than life.

14

ENDS OF THE
EARTH

EVERYTHING I TOUCH turns to dross. That is the ego-
ist's, as well as the realist's, version of my life. For every
place that I once loved and held in the center of my
heart has been taken from that velvet box and tossed onto the sidewalk for unheeding heels to crack and kick this way and that and
finally flatten into destruction. That's the way it looks from here.

When they built the Summit Mall—our first mall!—in my
hometown in 1965, it was set at the edge of the known world.
Previously one went back in time to shop, to the downtown department stores, but now we could go to the future. And what I liked
best about the drive to the mall was that not five minutes from

my house, after leaving the suburbs, we entered the country, and there was the sight of horses grazing open pasture before we reached that future. That was the way it was (town was town, country was country), and therefore that was the way it should be.

Then more of the future came and got the horses, and their homes became the front lawns of first Hampton Ridge, then Indian Hills, then Eagle's Chase and Greystone and Jennifer Street. The developments' names for some reason call forth the image of gel air freshener. Now I don't bother going the "back way" anymore to get to the mall (which is where I must go, as the downtown stores all closed within a year or two of the miraculous mall's appearance). I go the other way, boldly down Market Street and its constant loop replaying the same cheap melody: gas stations, groceries, shopping plazas, drugstores, quick lubes, doughnut shops, rotisserie chicken, bowling alleys. These are better than having to face the ghosts of horses grazing on the lawns of faux-stucco town houses.

I am a claustrophobe and malcontent, literally and poetically, both. I thus join a long line of pastoralists bemoaning the replacement of what once was by what has come to be. Oh, to have lived in Wordsworth's time, when vistas unsullied by man's touch poured themselves before the delighted eye. Then again, in Wordsworth's time, the encroaching manmade destroyer called the railroad caused him to cry out in alarm: "Is then no nook of English ground secure / From rash assault?" Dreams are the land we live on. If someone starts yammering about the good old days, my eyebrow rises of its own accord; but don't touch my childhood, which *was* the golden age.

The world's population has doubled in my lifetime, so far, and the knowledge makes my chest tight; what is gone is gone, and I have been made to watch its going. The northeast corner of my state—precious homeland—is now one continuous housing and shopping development, and what for me is an instinct residing at the depth of those for sleep or food, the need to drive to where you can be rid of all that and breathe once more, can never be sated there again. It is gone.

So is farmland everywhere, at the rate of two acres every minute. What kind of fact is that, one your mind won't grasp? (A million acres a year is no easier.) You will have to be satisfied by looking around your own backyard and extrapolating. To the extent of the known world.

The act will be corroborated by your readings. There's a news article from *The Guardian* titled "Humans Destroying the Natural World," and the first paragraph reads, in simplicity that defies paraphrase, "Humans have destroyed more than 30 percent of the natural world since 1970 with serious depletion of the forest, freshwater and marine systems on which life depends."

It shrinks and shrivels as you sleep, to wake the next morning in a smaller place than the day before, and the day before that. But escape is possible. You are certain, because you have been shown the way: Get into your shiny eighteen-foot sports-utility vehicle and it will lead you straight to a mountain byway amazingly devoid of any restrictions where you can climb and climb so to reach the top of the world and a timeless view of primeval wonders. That is where the natural world exists now.

Other scenes are equally persuasive that everything is the way it once was, only more so. Horses are central figures in these pictures, where we see that the family farm is still the happily expansive place of yore, only now greatly improved by a good insurance policy (or was that an antihistamine?). There are, as the commercial evidence proves, vast tracts of western landscape over which thundering herds of majestic mustangs move in a single ballet on the theme of freedom. And nothing will make one freer than that certain truck or cigarette or cologne or pair of jeans.

Forget the horse as symbol of dominion, power, or wealth. In the latter half of the twentieth century, it came to embody freedom, but especially Freedom, that American construct made up of equal parts Manifest Destiny, grit, hubris, and blindness. There is no better exemplar of a nation of restless movers than a horse whose range for four hundred years was as big as the imagination.

THERE MUST BE about 11,200 books targeted to kiddies who love horses, and I read most of them. They were as expendable as bubblegum (at least, once it has been chewed for the full forty-five minutes), although thirty years after first reading it, I discovered that the little blue-and-white paperback *More Horse Stories* had so deeply screwed itself into my brain that I could close my eyes and finish every line in the book.

But the Shakespeare of the genre, we all recognized, was Marguerite Henry. Hers were books you would save up for and buy in hardcover, some with jackets bearing an embossed gold sticker to show they had won an important award. Parents picked up on the rays of desire emanating from their progeny toward these volumes and, if they were the least bit caring, fulfilled the desire at least once.

My older sister received *King of the Wind,* the story of the Godolphin Arabian, one of the three foundation sires of the Thoroughbred. Its color pictures opened onto an exotic world, all turbans and tassels and djellabas. It was a page-turner, as were all of Marguerite Henry's books, for she was a master of the dash of danger, the soupçon of flavorful character, the cup of moral rectitude.

But the one my parents gave to me seemed more an omen than a gift; it was a signed copy, with a legible signature and signature horseshoe in felt-tip pen on the title page. The book was *Mustang, Wild Spirit of the West*. It contained one of the few Henry female protagonists, and its equine star for once was not an individual but a whole race of endangered animals.

I did not necessarily identify with Velma Johnston, the real-life heroine, although when she was described as a little girl who had to wear a body cast for months due to polio—as near to my harrowingly dread fear of being buried alive as I could stand to read about—I made myself think I could feel what she felt. But it was when Velma grew up, on the verge of transforming herself into Wild Horse Annie, that I felt the punch of identification—with the horses, that is—right in my gut, and it knocked the wind out of me.

The book describes how the young woman was driving near her Nevada ranch when she noticed something about the slat-sided truck in front of her: It was dripping blood. She followed it to the rendering plant, thinking how could anyone treat cattle or sheep that way, and as a good western girl who had grown up with horses for friends, she was shocked to see that horses were what the truck contained: wild horses packed as if to presage their upcoming future as the contents of a can. The detail omitted from the children's book version of this transformational event was that the blood was flowing largely from one source, the body of a colt who had been caught under the hooves of this truckload of frenzied animals. Even without it I felt a bit faint. It was worse when I got to the part where it showed how the wild ones were hunted down, with planes and trucks and hundred-pound tires lassoed around their necks. There was a burning in my lungs and incredulity in my heart; how could they? How could anyone? This was beyond anything that had ever occurred to me as possible, and I wanted to believe, as the book's ending said, that Wild Horse Annie had succeeded in her crusade to save the American wild horse—after all, there was now a law with her name on it, and one declaring the mustang a National Heritage species. That would make them too important to ever be killed again. Once people *knew* what had happened to these brave and beautiful creatures, they could never again countenance the carnage that had almost wiped them from the land. Because once people knew something, they could never again pretend they didn't know.

I STARTED TO HAVE dreams about the collision of bays and chestnuts and duns with the sidewalks. With modern urbanity, I mean.

I am standing in the circular drive, under a portico, of a fancy old hotel in Manhattan. Suddenly, out of the drive and onto the avenue bursts a vivid copper horse, being galloped up the street into the oncoming traffic. He is wildly reined this way and that in order to avoid the yellow cabs, then is turned away down a side street, where his impeccably clad rider performs a trick in which he slides Indian-style down his horse's side finally to cling insect-like underneath his barrel. But he seems to have trouble getting back up to the saddle like he should, and his bewildered mount slows to a trot. Somehow I reach them and begin yelling at him about the prodigious dangers of galloping a horse on hard pavement, into a menacing stream of cars. But what I have apparently not understood is that for this older gentleman's generation it was the tradition for men to ride to their offices, and he is merely the last in New York to follow its fine ways.

Another night I look out upon the dark street from a window. I hear hooves clipping the pavement, and into view ride a man and a woman on two horses. The riders are beautifully turned out in buff-colored breeches, black boots, velvet hunt caps. They wheel their animals around as they proceed to smash the windshields of every parked car in sight with vigor. I am sorely perplexed: Nice horsey young ladies don't *do* things like that! Underneath the confusion, though, is something worse, something weighing down my sleep like rocks. These horses must live in a city stable, and their world now is all pavement.

WE ARE HEMORRHAGING open space, but we have figured out a way to ease the loss. Symbols, unlike land, fit into shopping carts. And although wild horses in the true wild are not long for this world—the eradication campaign in the United States is headed by the government at the behest of the cattle ranchers' cabal, under the faultless guise of necessary population control; in Namibia, the feral horse population is dying from drought, and in other places the stories are different, but always end the same—domestics are adaptable enough to feed the hunger for the great yonder and the uplifting sight of its ground-eating denizens. There are now 5.32 million horses in this country, up more than 50,000 from the year before. Equestrian housing developments—ride your horse right past the front door of your mansion, which is guarded by sentries outside the electronic gate—are being advertised in every locale. One feed producer is opening by the dozen the type of fancified country store it has envisaged will cater to "ruralpolitan" markets, and boarding stables and riding camps are full up. They can't build stalls fast enough. We are living in horsey times indeed.

THE PRIZE WINNER

15

LEARNING CURVE

I WALKED UP barren Broadway from the subway station in the cold, Van Cortlandt Park's vast flat playing fields rolled out on my right. I kept going, lugging my suede shopping bag containing high boots, helmet, sweater. Then the sidewalk passed under a bridge and the entrance ramps to the Henry Hudson Parkway, and lo! Upon emerging from the spell of the dank rust, I saw that the countryside had been transported entire to this odd end of the city. How could it not make the heart of a horse lover leap? Look—barns, and paddocks, and a big red enclosed arena. I walked toward them over a field, and some horses in their blankets glanced up impassively at me.

I followed a sign that read OFFICE and found myself in the viewing room of the arena, which contained an old couch, some wooden benches, a TV and VCR, and a wood-burning stove. Beyond, through the window, people were riding. People and dogs lounged in the room watching them, eating chocolate cake that had been brought by someone. I had gotten here on the subway, and I was in the Bronx.

My teacher, Edith, took an instant dislike to me. That meant I immediately started feeling hopeless and defeated. And submission brings out aggression in a number of species, ours, unfortunately for me, included. She looked like an angry grown-up Heidi—long white-blonde hair, creamy skin, white knit band around her ears and under her ponytail. There was a hard ridge of exasperation under every word she spoke, and she was most critical of my rigidity, which meant I was hurting the horse every time I attempted to sit the trot. But her criticism increased my stiffness; it was a mounting circle of impossibility for me to try to relax when I was bracing myself against her sharp words. Most of all, I regretted what had initially seemed to me a good idea: To demonstrate that I was the kind of person who appreciated good instructors, I told her that I had had a gifted instructor in the summer. That immediately bristled her. Then, when she saw I was not exactly an inspired rider, and also had the gall to offer a bit of wisdom that her face instantly showed was contrary to her own, she determined that not only did I have a terrible instructor, I was so stupid I could not even tell the difference between an idiot and its opposite number.

The second lesson went barely better. My mistake this time, apart from being a hopeless bore as a student, was to attempt to open a conversation on a subject that had lately been intruding more and more on my thoughts: What right do I assume in using this animal to learn to ride? I mean, what does he get out of it? Is there not a compact implicit in his relative helplessness and our ability to profit from it, one that can never be fulfilled for the school horse and that thus makes him no better than a slave?

Her eyes signaled her desire that I should fall off the horse and break a large and important bone so that I would never come back to torment her for any other half hour.

WEEKS LATER, I HAVE almost begun to dread going riding. It is decidedly not fun. It is not only Edith that acts as aversion therapy; it is the whole place, the whole of the Riverdale establishment. I am an alien thing blowing in there once a week, a gnatlike annoyance so small they do not address me but absentmindedly brush me away by reflex. You see, I don't fit into any of the known categories: cute, willing horse-loving child; teenage up-and-coming rider-athlete who lives and breathes horses and thus Riverdale; wealthy woman with coddled horse, who is pumping twelve hundred dollars a month for board and lessons into the operation. I am the kind of rider who, viewed by the gallery of critics on the other side of the viewing-room glass, grading performance ("she's such an elegant rider"; "look at those spurs she has on—they're like daggers, and the horse is *still* poking along"; "she's not a pretty rider, but she's taught him every move he has"), might prompt a grimace. I'm worth thirty dollars a week to them. I take the subway in a three-and-a-half-hour round trip to fight with an aged, lame pony named Cloudy and get yelled at. But—and this is the funny part—I am improving. I felt, for the first time last week, what it was like to post naturally, rising with the impulsion of the horse. *And,* a week before that, I figured out what it really means to ask the horse to halt using your seat: Just a little indelicately put, you tighten the muscles across your gut as if you were about to push to   Well, maybe that's not right, but it worked.

SCENES THROUGH THE GLASS

The well-to-do mother and daughter taking lessons at the same time. Little girl beginning on a longe-line pony; slender attractive mom cantering around and around. She knows what she's doing on a horse. She has brought her daughter here to attain the same graceful skills.

Another well-to-do woman—this one obviously even richer (and thinner) than the aforesaid mom. Her own white horse, fastidiously groomed with long flowing tail, looks like a Maserati among the VWs out there—making me realize I am myself a rusty International truck with my scrubby attire (I own two pairs of breeches all told, no whip, my sister's old helmet, which has fallen in manure more than once, and the cheapest leather boots currently on the market) astride the limping, urine-stained Cloudy. This lady is wearing a cashmere sweater tucked into impeccably fitting breeches; her boots are clearly custom-made. Everything looks like she cut the tags off this morning, especially the black dressage saddle and snow-white dressage pad edged in black. She is not, however, a "pretty rider."

An overheard discussion between the stable owner—a former Olympic rider—and a guy with a forehead like a granite overhang, wearing sneakers and a full-length black leather trench coat: He wants to buy or lease a horse for the girl who's out in the ring—his daughter?—and is told a full lease costs one thousand dollars a month. He does not flinch.

IN LATE FEBRUARY, serendipity smiled on me, in the form of its frown on sour Edith. I was informed that my lesson this week would be taught by Lee Ann; Edith had broken her leg in a skiing accident. Lee Ann reminds me of the sort of sunny all-I-wanna-do-is-have-some-fun girl with whom my little sister is often friends—she is probably in her early twenties, many years my junior. Even on poor old Cloudy I did better, from sheer relief. Then the next week I was given Belle to ride, and suddenly, with a new horse and a new teacher, I felt my enthusiasm come back. Belle is a small, rotund dappled roan with white stockings, and she is seven years old—a youngster among these ancient sages. I was warned that if she put her head down, prelude to bucking, not to put up with it for one minute, and so chastened, she would settle down. It happened exactly as foretold, and then she seemed more or less okay with me being on top of her and asking her to do things. Not thrilled, but okay. And I didn't feel I was abusing a senior citizen by riding her. Lee Ann was encouraging, and though I still gave her plenty of faults to correct, I felt that I was not just one big insupportable exasperation to my teacher.

The following week, the weather was so amiable when I arrived that Lee Ann asked if I wanted to work in the outside ring. It is a clay surface demarcated by railroad ties, with a few cavalletti and rails lying on the ground in the center. All started fine; it was great to be outdoors with "my" Belle, whom I had very quickly decided to "love," my head filled with fantasy nonsense.

Then we started working on walk-trot transitions, very quickly switching back and forth. After the tenth request to trot after only one or two steps of walk, Belle got mad. *To hell with this!* and she kick-bucked out to the side. That little dance interrupting the peace was like a door swinging open in my mind where I had thought there was only imperturbable wall: and I saw into the new dark space to discover that just beyond was the possibility of serious misbehavior. Misbehavior from a thousand pounds of headstrong muscle, with open fields and roadway to right, haven of barn to left. The only thing left to learn was which it would be.

Halfway around the small circle at a canter (a gait that I craved as a child but now rather frightens me), Belle decided she'd had enough of this crap, too, and she took off toward the left. I heard Lee Ann yelling, "Right! Right!" and I halfheartedly tried to aim Belle right, while my heart wanted to capitulate and let her go around left, thinking I'd get her settled down sometime later (I know, I know, it doesn't work that way with horses). I wanted to *commune* with her, not *correct* her. The net effect of my dillydallying was that she went straight, right toward a jump.

Okay, so the thing was not the Budweiser bottle five-footer at the Grand Prix; it's one foot, maybe one and a half if I'm lucky. My childhood lessons in jumping had painted it a strictly point-and-shoot affair—give her her head, attach your hands to the mane halfway up the neck, and get out of the saddle. No big deal. I am reminded once again of why jumping becomes so addictive: It is a literal rush, no time to savor the sensation of a huge force rising under you and carrying you along with its sheer implacability, but just enough time to develop the urge to put another quarter in the slot.

After I landed, Lee Ann remarked, "Boy, if it was me I'd have just bailed out—I hate jumping." (No way, I thought immediately: For one thing, that was barely jumping, and for another, it didn't really scare me, and it's not possible for anyone to be scared of something that doesn't scare me.) I figured she was humoring me, but she reiterated, "No, I mean it. I jumped *all* the time as a kid, but now it scares me."

But I had engineered a precarious position for myself, on top of a horse that had really made up her mind to get out of this place. And it was I who blithely offered her the secret decoder ring so that she could get the information she needed to procure her end. At a trot, she suddenly veered outside toward the barn, but I pulled and circled her right back in. I was too scared now to canter—speed, coupled with my increased flopping around, made me feel the potential for a real running-away scene.

As I dismounted, Lee Ann told me that I had done well; that I was strong enough to make Belle rethink her position. And instead of feeling like I had failed, and that a better rider would never have found herself in remotely the same situation, I realized: No, this is what riders have to do all the time. Riding doesn't mean going around in placid circles continuously—it sometimes means "showing who's boss." And you don't get that opportunity unless the animal acts up first. After all, didn't Lee Ann just tell me she had earlier ridden some fourteen-year-old girl's gray, whom I had petted as he had stood innocent in the crossties, and had had a terrible row with him? Maybe she even looked—just a little, vague bit—like me.

But *boss*? This is not a suit that will likely ever fit. And it is the only one at the store when I go looking for riding clothes. I watch the admirable women take charge, a smart whack from a crop at the first sign of disobedience, and no residual fear, because, after all, *who* is riding whom? I listen to Edith yell, "When I tell you to use the whip, you must *use the whip*." I am thinking of giving up.

IN APRIL LEE ANN got sick, and I got Edith again. And you know what? She was the picture of calm. I had a wonderful lesson, learning the rudimentaries of the indirect rein. She told me it is the way to control a horse from running out on you—a horse like Belle. (My love for Belle was brief but pure; she was the first horse I'd ridden at Riverdale who seemed to have any spirit left in her at all. Then one day Lee Ann said, "Belle? Belle's a *cow*.")

Lee Ann left. I didn't realize she was just there on a layover, before she resumed the accelerating trajectory of her life. She was off to be with a friend who was riding in the World Cup, then back home to Canada. During the summer she would go to Germany to train with Canada's Olympic coach—she'd been shortlisted for the team. (How wonderful, I thought, to turn on the TV one day and see her there and be able to say, "She was my instructor!" at which incredulous looks would shoot my way.) She is, in fact, twenty years old, with life a mystery before her. I suppose it's one in front of me, too, but often I feel that I know every dry wrinkle in it, and when it doesn't bore or scare me, it goes by too fast to feel.

I revisit my summer haunts, and I call to take a lesson with Dominique. It turns out to be a very mixed bag—when all I thought I would feel was relief and pleasure. Well, she's careful, that you can say about her. She put me on the longe line again, saying that Wilant had lately become a bit feisty since he was doing more serious dressage work. That and the fact that the cold air of March really wakes them up. (So the stolid school horses at Riverdale must act like bronze statues in August.) She immediately claims that I'm even worse now than I was when I first began, that she would have thought I'd be improved if I was riding every week, and that since I'm not I must have been instructed improperly and am developing bad habits that will be even harder to break than if I had simply not ridden at all. When she hears that I've been cantering, she hits the roof, saying it is utterly wrong, practically malpractice for them to have me cantering when I can't hold my body together at the trot. Well, I have already paid for four more lessons at Riverdale, and when they tell you to canter, you *canter*.

And so I will return to my teachers, and I will try to make amends. I will also try to overcome a stiff body, a negative mind, and a tendency to think too much about something that yields so little to thinking. It was never this complicated before.

16

WHAT IS THIS
THING CALLED

G O BACK ONCE MORE to when they are little girls, to when they use all powers of mind and musculature to become horses themselves. (If there is something called lycanthropy, then this is surely equianthropy.) When they grow up, the imprint remains on them, a part of their bones and their cells and the beautiful braids and twists and beads that make up the substance that makes up their cells. Women are already more like horses than they know.

Their inner ears, for one, are able to detect very soft sounds better than men's. They are alert to peril, and especially to the sounds of whimpering in the depths of night, from way down the hall, a sound that to them might as well be the porcelain lamp smashing into a thousand bits and to their snoring husbands might as well be nothing. Now look at the horse: Aren't the ears one of the first things you notice? The way they swivel robotically, sensitive as sonar to the otherwise unheard pin drop down the aisle, or down the miles.

Although the horse is kept in his stable, fenced in by the electric tape of his paddock and by his paddock's own limits, beyond which are now shopping centers and roads and houses and very few rocky crags, he still remembers with his blood what it was like to feel the sudden weight of four paws landing heavy and quiet on his back, the closely following embrace of unsheathed claw under the skin of his withers. The memory of the mountain lion is borne somehow down the generations so that when you go into his stall you will find (a hundred years after the last carnivore was pictured hanging limply over the shoulder of his proud, smiling conqueror), when you raise the broom overhead to bring down the cobwebs from the rafters, an animal suddenly white-eyed with terror, shuffing breath in a frantic tempo through distended nostrils. Now look at the woman, who finds her respiration going ahead without her as she walks through the shadows, and who doesn't want to look behind her for fear of making material the very thing she fears, so she walks a little faster. She knows, too (says horse listener Monty Roberts), what it is like to be prey.

THE FIFTEENTH-CENTURY MYSTIC Margery Kempe saw a man striking a horse, and as she stared the image dissolved. Its particles reformed and there before her was Christ being lashed, his blood flowing like tears.

To blasphemously put her beloved Christ's face where before there was only a beast's (only, certainly, the very least of his brethren)—this, as we have come to see, is rank sentimentality, woman's foolishness. We are supposed to be civilizing ourselves out of it, but there is one slight problem: That sentimentality, also known as compassion, is the one thing that has allowed human civilization to continue, for without it we would leave our children hungry in the streets and our babies tied to tables to learn (for science is civilization minus compassion) how long it takes them to expire from neglect. As the British critic Brigid Brophy, who has the knack of seeing this clearly, has written: "Whenever people say 'We mustn't be sentimental,' you can take it they are about to do something cruel. And if they add 'We must be realistic,' they mean they are going to make money out of it."

What other than some form of compassion, however admixed (always, always) with its opposite, can explain those women who can do with a horse what no one else can do? The young Dorothy Herbert, circus trainer of long ago, whose charges all had the tendency to be dangerous (they required the propensity to rear) and whose Satan could not be sat by anyone but her, but for her would—and did—walk through fire; the famous competitor of the sixties Kathy Kusner, whose Aberali was described as "too nervous to take a bit in his mouth—he must wear only a hackamore—and yet Kathy's got him acting as though he wants to get on his knees and thank her every time he takes a jump." What other than "sentimentality" facing down "realism" recently caused a former college student to take out a loan for $720 that she is going to have trouble paying back so she could buy the seventeen-year-old jumper she had ridden in equitation class out from the hands of the meat dealer? (And what an example to realists everywhere the professor who sent him to the auction, proud enough of his high degree of civilized unsentimentality to remark on the record, "It's strictly a business decision.")

Whippers, beaters, abusers, sadists, those whose compassion has suffered a fatal leak and left the bucket dry—all are found among the ranks of women who profess to love horses (just as women, those natural nurturers, actually kill children at a rate far greater than men do). But there are just enough of the others— the deeply understanding, the quietly caring—among these women, too, coupled with too many stories of preternatural affection to be happenstance, that we must try again to comprehend the evidence.

Maybe it is that the desire to be with horses and their warm breath and trusting natures is most basically the desire to feel love—profound, joyous, irreducible love—and especially that rare breed of it that one feels only for offspring. If in their dependent state domesticated horses are like children (and who are we to ignore the voices of those thousands of women who say they are?), then they must be triggering the finally inexplicable instincts that blind us to the particular shape of our charges—whether they are covered in brown hair or pink skin, or have our eyes or those of someone on another continent—and cause us to love them with a fierceness that is almost embarrassing. Because mothers do not *choose* to love their babies, as if they had considered the merits of their intelligence or beauty or potential and found them sufficient; they love them rather because biology has insisted they do, and what is in our cells goes deeper than what is in our minds. Why try to keep it secret that this love is so delicious that we crave it with as powerful a hunger as it is possible to feel without going mad?

And maybe there is something else, too (I assure you, there is always something else). We are attracted to horses, in particular, because they echo our own tentative whispers but do so in a bold, ringing call; they speak with certainty of exactly those things we are most unsure of in ourselves. For the qualities that most define the equine species are the ones most suppressed currently in the human: raw sexuality, fear, open vulnerability and need, uncomplicated drive. They want only to live, which is to say to fulfill their biologically ordained needs (to feel safe, to commune with others of their kind, to move and play and create life). This reminds us of what we have forgotten about ourselves, and it is enough to make us want to cry. And enough, perhaps, to make tears stop.

AS IF TO SHOW that it is all beyond the pithless ability of words to explain, the artists have taken up the flag. Rosa Bonheur (1822–1899) had at least one great painting in her, animated by an intensity of sensuous feeling ("Oh, those suggestive hindquarters . . ." in the words of one of today's many painters working the suggestive area of horse art) as well as an intensity of moral feeling. The painter of the monumental *Horse Fair* once did rely on words to explain what she thought about the animal that gave her her best subject:

> The horse is, like man, the most beautiful and the most miserable of creatures, only, in the case of man, it is vice or property that makes him ugly. He is responsible for his own decadence, while the horse is only a slave that the Creator has given to man, who abuses it out of his ingratitude and his worldly and egoistic poverty, until he becomes lower than the animal itself.

Nothing as simple as beauty or misery is the issue for the late-twentieth-century women who have found the horse and our relationship with it to be thick ground for art that goes where words cannot. Deborah Butterfield makes sculptures, sometimes life-sized, out of bent sticks or rusted debris that economically sketch against the background of air the exact gestures of live horses so uncannily that you are forced to think on the sort of high-flown subjects best accessed through simplicity: the nature of animation and creation; the hand of man and that of something more hidden from our eyes. Susan Rothenberg claims no special concern for horses as horses, only as figurative elements that keep getting pushed over into abstraction, yet every essence of horseness has played a role in her consistent use of them over the course of many years. Her horses look helpless as they are about to be pulled into some dark and endless vortex, spinning in space as if they were weightless, which makes us a little uncomfortable, since when is a horse helpless or weightless? Deborah Bright takes photographs of horsey accoutrements—slick leather saddles, model horses enchained—to make various comments on lust, slavery, and the slavery of lust; one series is titled "Being and Riding." Patricia Cronin copies, in bright blocks of color that recall paint-by-numbers, images from the vast supply of horse porn that arrives in monthly installments of some of the magazines: the centerfolds of majestic breed exemplars, the ads in which a young woman shares a moment of secluded bliss with her mount. Wendy Klemperer sculpts industrially energetic horses, and she has also made a telling video in which naked women, their privates covered only by fluttering show ribbons, jump a course as if they were horses while simultaneously acting as riders. (After viewing it you will never again innocently read the line in *National Velvet* in which the heroine flicks her own thigh with a switch as she canters.) And then there is Janet Biggs, whose video installations have directly taken on girls and horses using a complex of simultaneously running approaches to the already multivalent subject; together they create a sort of visual white noise in which the viewer can profitably wander and listen for a good long while.

Their work, as the best art has always done, poses questions instead of giving answers. In the end, we must be satisfied with this. It is something, anyway, that we can develop quite a desire for, if it happens not to appeal to us on first bite. I myself have become almost addicted to the taste of the unknowable, and sometimes gorge on it in the middle of the night, straight out of the container and with no sauce. With this relevation, I hereby give up all pretense of offering some final explanation of why girls love horses with the abiding passion they do. Instead, I invite you to the feast of uncertainty.

17

NARCISSIST

L ET'S GO RIDING!" A call, to the child, as irresistible as
"Let's eat ice cream for dinner, ride the roller coaster six
times, and stay up telling ghost stories all night!" And so
we'd go, wherever and whenever we could. Pony rides at the
fair—we'd line up for those for forty-five minutes under hot sun,
get plopped on the western saddle and told to hang on to the horn
(a barely endurable patronization to six-year-olds who believed
their education about the most beloved creature on earth to be
nearly complete), and for two desultory turns around the dusty
ring we were walking but in our minds preparing to lope off to
the canyonlands. We were pulled off too soon, mightily disap-

pointed in the whole affair, barely given enough time to pat the pony's nose while another hope-filled child was hoisted aboard, and still we'd run back to the end of the line, to our parents' exasperated expulsions of breath. On any family vacation we'd find where the trail rides were, and we wouldn't let up the kind of pinched-by-a-pliers pressure only a child knows how to apply on parents, until they cried uncle. We'd gladly walk in a line of fifteen others for a solemn hour, nose to tail to nose, our jaded steeds hoping only for a mouthful of leaves along the way and the end of it all. Then there was the constant clamor for lessons, the fearsome whining that was the vocal emanation of a volcano of desire. The sage parent recognized this as the useful lever it was, and could get virtually anything in return for acquiescence in the matter. (For instance, one girl's parents received several years of violently abhorred piano lessons and daily practice sessions.) "Let's go riding!" because it was, and is, an inimitable sensation, and no magic flying carpet can do it better.

The perennial staple of the travel supplement and women's magazine is the article by the middle-aged writer who has rediscovered exactly this past, the small ember that turned out to glow hotly when breathed upon by the otherwise innocent trail ride or city encounter with a horse. A variation is the author who has decided to confront a decades-old dislike of horses that is now recognized as having originated in fear. She catalogs her first day in the saddle, the racing heart, the understanding but strict tutor, the small but heady triumph of applying crop to rump with certitude and finally getting a few strides of trot. All the denizens of the stable are described as the individuals they are, usually by way of a compilation of evasions developed over the years: the one who at every chance heads to the middle of the arena to stand like stone; the one whose head tosses and tail switches through the whole lesson; the one who cannot, by any means, be roused from a hoof-dragging walk. There are depictions of the crates of apples bestowed on these four-legged teachers by grateful students, and some interesting facts, such as that a thirty-five-year-old is still being used for lessons, and that he has lived in the urban stable for twenty-five of those years. The piece winds on, charting the author's hard-won ascendancy to a rider who is in control of herself and proud of it. She can make an animal respond to her heels and her crop, and she extols the knowledgeable instructors and the amazing thing about the whole enterprise—that it is located a subway ride away.

Hurrah for her. But by the finish of your third or fourth or seventy-eighth piece like this, it has become difficult for you to echo its "Let's go riding!" with any previous enthusiasm. You have no idea where these sour-faced doubts came from, only that now they are perched with their claws dug into your shoulder and insist on reading along with you, whispering dry words through sharp teeth at every line. You realize that you are not going to get rid of this homunculus, either; he's here to stay. And simultaneously your pleasures have deflated as surely as the helium balloon tied at night to the bedpost with loving care that by morning lies wrinkled on the floor. Perhaps it has something to do with the fact that you were turned around at birth, facing the opposite way from the majority of others. The being's intractable little voice won't leave you alone, scratching at your ear: Isn't there something they left out? Twenty-five hundred words and not a single one from the point of view of the horses themselves? Do they not figure in this at all? "Let's go riding!" indeed. What if they *don't want to be ridden?*

EVERYTHING NOW HAS reversed itself and nothing is the same as it was. You begin to think you are like that little kid in the scary movie, the one who could see plain as day all those who had recently died from violent causes while everyone else went about their merry business, oblivious that they were knocking into bloody ghosts and treading on their shoes. So you can no longer read that piece and think, *Wow, twenty-five years in the same place doing the same thing—cool!* You will now think, *Jesus Christ, twenty-five years without tasting grass, without rolling on his back, without the simple necessity of moving his legs without the weight of a human bearing down and pulling him this way and that, twenty-five years in a cell. What did he do,* you will think, *to warrant a sentence of life in prison?* A rail car of apples and days of hugs can't pay him back for that; it's like locking a child up alone in a closet for years but making sure he has ample lollipops. You can no longer think, *Ha, ha, isn't that funny, that horse who turns to face the wall of the arena and won't budge for love or money.* Now you'll think, bile rising, *That's all we've left them with, their one attempt to turn off the incessant pain and boredom that goes on and on for them like a television tuned permanently to loud static.*

You know what you used to get out of it—the pleasure, the mastery, the wind in your face—but suddenly you've got to ask, because of that damned demon who seems to stay here to infect everything you once took for granted, what they get out of it. And if the answer is nothing that they would want more than the ful-fillment of the instincts that pull and pull at them until something has to give, then it doesn't matter what you want, because you've got all the power you need to fulfill your desires. And they have none. This is not a comfortable state of affairs anymore, you are sorry to report. You no longer want to be a party to it, even if it means giving up part of your past, or the opportunity to join this large community of others who are embraced by their joy and do not see the dark clouds over the horizon you seem to notice at every turn. It appears you have become an outsider, and all the other horsewomen are inside, warm.

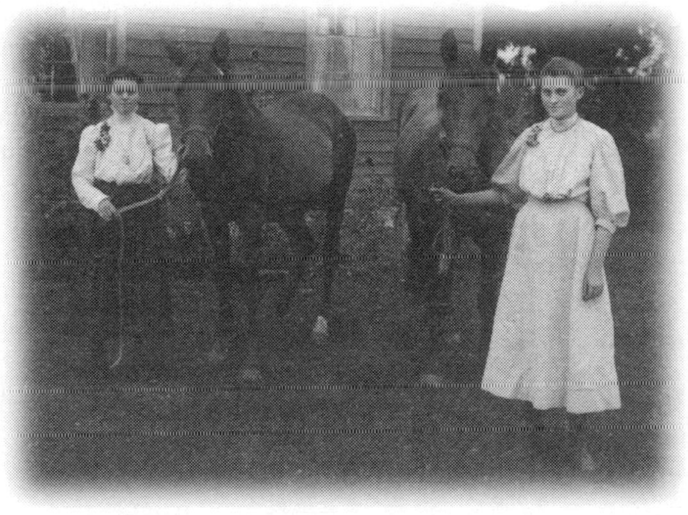

18

CRACK FORMING

THE SOUND OF THE slaps resounded through the arena, echoed off the high tin ceiling of the sacred space. Each was followed by a stream of parental invective: "Now *stop* that, mister." "If I even see—*even see*—those teeth of yours once more I'm going to make you sorry." "You know not to . . ."

A few seconds later, another *thwack,* another sermon in Monica's mellifluous tones.

She and her horse, a young and strapping Dutch warmblood (the breed of choice for every rider on the rise these days, the Lexus of horses), went through this routine every time they were together, he turning to pull at some bit of her clothing with his handsome teeth, she responding with a slap on his neck with her open palm and a foretaste of what she would be like as a mother. No matter how colorfully strident her remonstrances, her horse was apparently too thick to get it. His English language skills had failed to progress.

Every time I watched their pas de deux I was reminded of dog owners who keep crying "Come, Buster, *come*. Come, come!" as their dogs are running merrily away. Their calls arise from the bottom of a deep well into which they didn't even know they had fallen, unable to escape: the well of speech. If only someone could pass a law prohibiting the use of spoken language in animal training, or at least require alternates, such as *chair* for "sit," *rice* for "come." Then maybe people would realize they have to teach first, speak second. Or not at all—visual cues work just as well as verbal ones.

I wondered why Dominique did not inform Monica that if you have to rehearse the same play over and over again without ever getting to a real performance, it's the director's fault. Then again, knowing the financial role of Monica's fiancé in building this facility, as well as the natural recalcitrance of Monica's intellect to expand, I wasn't that surprised. Nonetheless, I remained appreciative of her wardrobe of trim breeches and the fact that she stood definitively on one side of the great divide: women whose hair stayed perfectly coiffed no matter what they did around horses, and women like me.

DOMINIQUE AND THE crowd at Riverdale struck me as single-minded in a way that I had never been about anything, and that made me wonder about what joys I might be missing out on. They could incline their heads toward one another and say some word no one else would understand and thereby exchange whole days' worth of meaning, triggering smiles or smirks that left everyone else outside the door. Dressage was their world; they could sit for hours and dismantle videos of Olympic performances until each pixel stood on its own. It was clear to me, watching, that some horses showed more floating brilliance in their movements, some riders had a lighter grace than others, but that was the extent of my discrimination. Then I would begin to wonder if the horses would rather be doing something else. When I watched the women live and at close hand working their mounts, I saw only the green-tinged foam fall back from the horses' lips onto the chests that were slowly darkening with sweat and I realized that I didn't really *get* it. It was their discipline, never to be mine. What was it really about? Inside and outside? Inhabiting a world with rules that are actually written in black and white in booklets put out by a governing agency? Inhabiting a world that is so intricate it fully engages you to the point that you forget the other one exists, its great stretches of quicksand and bad weather and little or no concrete guidance? They worked on their tests with relentless patience through the winter and waited, watching videos, for the show season to begin once more.

I merely waited, for what I did not know. Learning to ride was as it might have been predicted: good days and bad, flashes of revelation, some momentary freeing of the horse that allowed him to spring or stretch or reach into my hand, which felt so expansively like I had suddenly become a ballroom dancer at the top of my form that when it clunked inevitably into the following moment, when I couldn't coordinate anything and my back stiffened and my legs flailed and the horse set himself against me, it was plain sad. But the end of the lesson was the end of horses for the day, and the four-legged creatures went back to their real jobs—chewing, the avocation they take in dead earnest—and the two-leggeds to theirs—providing them with something to chew.

Dominique and the others had found the place they wanted to live and they lived there, a foreign land. I was still reading guide books, trying to picture what places might exist so I would want to journey there.

I LIVE IN A STATE of permanent longing, a creek bed so deeply carved that the periodic gratifications cannot hope to divert the flow. And the longest practice session in my life devoted to unrequited longing was the time I spent wanting a horse. My final acceptance, at a young age, of the impossibility of having one caused me to turn away with resolute bitterness. Very well, then, I *will not* have a horse! The next twenty years were spent in a universe that had never known that peculiarly sharp and trenchant odor that clings to your hands after a day at the stables. Save, that is, for the one fluke of a Thanksgiving Day when a high school friend invited me on her family's traditional cross-country ride and offered me their pony. Knowing just what to do with a sort such as me, midway through he reconquered the bit and ran like hell. I remember thinking I should circle him, but we were on a narrow trail at the edge of cornfields. I imagined him breaking a leg in the plow lines. So I held on, until he reached the blacktop. Traffic was relatively light that day. I don't recall what part of me hit first, because I blacked out for a moment. The fear of what I might see as I rolled myself over on the road is something I do remember well. But the pony was back on his feet, a broken girth dangling, a knee skinned, dazed by his fortune.

Then I went back to the pale, horseless world.

19

COUNTERINDICATIONS

A T THE NATIONAL HORSE SHOW, recently returned from several years of humiliation in an arena in New Jersey to its former center-of-the-universe glory in Manhattan's Madison Square Garden, it is possible to see (in retrospect) a prefiguration of the event in the place for prefiguration, the lobby. There, outside the entrance, a dejectedly lone Budweiser Clydesdale is on display in what could only be called a cage. Crowds of people press close to see what is inside and raise children up to see and push their fingers inside the bars. I feel certain I have seen exactly this scene in a Grandville cartoon.

As the ticket holders flow upriver on escalators, they can look out wide expanses of glass to the streets below and see, as usual, the Friday night traffic progressing by inches, only tonight horse trailers are among the stalled and smoking cabs and trucks. I remember overhearing Dominique remark to someone, months before, when the venue change was announced, "Well, isn't that all the proof you need they don't give a damn about their horses?" I didn't quite understand until now.

Dotting the audience inside are large clots of girls, ten or twelve to a group, many prepubescent and sporting identical windbreakers embroidered with the image of a horse over the name of their stable. They are all on the same team. They run up and down the aisles like a stream of mercury that breaks into beads and rejoins itself constantly, clutching their programs, finding a big enough block of seats to sit together as one, turning first toward this one then toward that, talking excitedly, earnestly, in double time.

The course for international team jumping is being set up, and it is a succinct and nuanced representation of the concept of impossibility. The jumps are so closely spaced, I imagine the horses having to launch themselves from a virtual standstill. At the first horse's round, an entry from Sweden, my heart begins to pound loudly even though I have no particular affection for Sweden. A few horses later and I have been given reason to fear, at least the water jump, since more of them have trouble here than anywhere else. One slipped just before and went smashing through the double bars.

The Maclay competition allows me to calm somewhat, as the jumps have not been imported from the underworld. Instead, this looks closer to ballet than to the shotput of Grand Prix, and the riders—the top eleven are all young women—look as light as film on the backs of their mounts, not one of them wrestling with her horse's mouth or ratcheting him around a frightfully tight line so as to save a precious sliver of a second.

Every horse in every class shows its personality—some can't stand still, others appear mentally transported to calmer shores. One lashes out with his hind legs over each jump, apparently not in happiness. A couple put on a brief Wild West rodeo before being persuaded to keep all four hooves on the ground. Some definitely do not want a ribbon pinned to their bridles and waltz at arm's length with the steward assigned to give them one. I hear a woman behind me say with a laugh, "They'll jump the most formidable obstacle the world has ever seen, but a ribbon—*oh, no!*" Actually, the problem is a patch of light on the ground thrown by the spots; it might as well be a hole into eternity they are being asked to step into.

After a break for a soft pretzel with mustard, I find a new seat, this time in front of one of the aforementioned gaggle of girls. These, I later find out, are from Stoneleigh-Burnham, a girls' boarding school in western Massachusetts where you can even take some academic classes along with your rigorous program of riding. I overhear one saying, "My boyfriend *knows* I would give him up in a flash for my horse—that's the way it is, and that's the way it's always going to be." Another rejoins, "Well, *I* left home so I could be with horses instead." As they watch the course being set up for the next Grand Prix class, one says in a voice dripping with envy, "Oh, man, I wish we had these jumps at school!" and her friend agrees: "Me and Gilligan are *ready* for these jumps." She pauses while a thought comes to her. "Actually, Gilligan is so smart he'd try to go *under* them."

When the Saddlebreds appear in the ring, the girls become indignant. "You know how they get them to do that stuff—it's disgusting. They cut their pasterns or the quick of their hooves, and they put crap on the wounds and everything." They sit back with their arms folded against their chests and are silent except for the occasional expulsion. "I mean, yuck!" "Look at that—they think that's pretty? He's practically bugging out with fear." The horses fly around the ring, throwing their knees up to their chins, sweat staining their forehands. Their eyes show white.

As the same thing goes on in the Arabian pleasure-horse class, it occurs to me that these animals are the equine equivalent of the anorexic girl who starves herself in order to replicate the kind of fashion-model ideal that could never exist in nature, but that is derived from artistic romanticizations of nature going back to Beardsley. They are horses made to move in a way that imitates only the hyperbolic horse of legend—fiery, barely of this earth. If the tail doesn't assume the aspect of the wind-whipped stallion out on the steppes, why then break and reset it so it does. Right then and there I formulate my theories, and it is a good thing I have a notebook so as to record such magnitudinous revelations. "Underlying such transformations are two things: a (self)-loathing for the way things *are,* and the belief that human intervention is required by just about everything that doesn't have anything, really, to do with the human—the urge toward colonization." The sight appalls me, when it is supposed to entrance me with its grace.

PEOPLE WHO BELIEVE women are not naturally competitive have obviously never been to a horse show. Just look around at the grim faces, at the warm-up ring where the same two jumps are gone over again and again, until the horse's exasperated inability to understand what is asked of him (in fact, it is perfection) results in the irony of diminishing performance. In the actions of others, you can read such a strict resistance to losing that no such backfiring is allowed. Only concentration, concentrated concentration. There may, in fact, be nothing in nature or society fiercer than a woman in the grips of a desire to win. Look how badly they want it: See there a rider with a broken ankle, taped tightly enough for her to compete, though not enough to erase the pain she feels every time she puts weight on the injury, which is approximately every twelve seconds; see one of the top Grand Prix riders in the world enter a show though her face is a mass of purple bruises, her nose is broken, and her head has swelled three sizes. It is not really a joke, that T-shirt that reads, "My husband told me if I went to another horse show he was going to leave me. I'm sure going to miss him."

One woman who began riding at five but whose parents' divorce when she was fifteen made her sell her horse reports that it caused lasting psychological damage. In college she caught sight of the cover of a magazine picturing a friend of hers as the winner of a big show, and she burst into sobs of jealousy. So when she married rich—big-time rich—she knew exactly what she was going to do. With her children left in the care of the nanny, she went back into training with a suitably competitive horse. Using parlance familiar to any recovering addict, she says she couldn't stop herself; she became more passionate about her horse and the lure of winning than she was about her husband. For his part, he told her he didn't want to become "one of those schmucks who stand around holding the reins for their wives." Until counseling, it looked as though she would repeat her parents' history.

On a related subject, she has a quick answer to a bewildering question: How, when such intense trust and partnership between horse and rider is required in order to achieve at the upper levels of competition, could a rider consider killing a horse for the insurance money? It happens often enough: barn fire, anal electrocution, a crowbar to the knee. It is extreme wealth, she says, that instills aberrant values: "It exists for my pleasure, and if I am no longer pleased with it, kill it." A horse becomes no different than a boat or car or kitchen renovation. Some sort of aberrant value, at any rate, was operating the day another show competitor contested the size of an entry in a pony class, whereupon the enraged owner had the horse killed. The same might be said for a more routine occurrence on the show circuit—the rampant use of drugs to enable horses to continue going over those same two jumps, again and again and again, until the rider has it just right. Congregating around the tents of every upper-level show are the veterinarians who for $175 will let your horse have a hit from their magic syringe.

And since you knew it was coming, I will be brief with another bit of bad news, this directed to the wishful fantasies of those legions of hopeful young ladies who flock to the racetracks to be with the ones they love: Flat racing is hardly innocent either, which you already knew deep in your heart, because you know what large quantities of money do, are helpless but to do, corrupting everything but the purity of the money. (The Quakers were onto racing as long ago as the mid-seventeenth century, condemning it for "overstraining . . . and over-forcing creatures . . . beyond their strength.")

Racing, already inherently harmful or "destructive to the creatures," has become increasingly more so, with the great majority of Thoroughbreds suffering ulcers, bleeding lungs, and injuries due to working too early, breeding for light bones, and, especially, the use of pain-masking drugs (at one track in West Virginia, the number of horses that had to be euthanized upon breaking down doubled from an average of thirty per year to sixty after the legalization of phenylbutazone). Thousands who can't make a buck go to slaughterhouses every year; up to 75 percent of all racehorses will end that way—and large-scale overbreeding makes it cost-effective. In England it is no better: More than one hundred horses are killed annually on British tracks; dozens of horses have been done in at the Aintree Grand National, three of them in 1998. I came across an interesting article in *Horse & Hound* about British steeplechase jockey Gee Armytage and her will to win, so fervent it caused her to be rather profligate with the stick; her brother recounted with amusement how at the beginning of her career she used it "usually once a stride and everywhere on the horse between its ears and tail once it began to tire." Thus the horse's reward for giving everything. Some horses do indeed enjoy jumping and running (and some do not), but it is hard to imagine what incentive they might claim to do it to the point of death. People who have closely observed wild horse behavior describe how the ultimate fee is never demanded of a horse who doesn't himself offer it; in a fight there is always an out, a way to say "I quit" that is respectfully honored. We are the ones who demand that the natural order be suspended. And so they continue to run on broken legs, until the heart bursts, to the edge of collapse. For a ribbon, a cup, our pride, and a sizable check.

COMPETITION IS A way to get more deeply into the bond, and, as we already know, the bond is already a drug, the heroin of life. For all that they contend horses are like children, to the women who ride them, horses are something else. They are not only dependent creatures to be taken care of, they are also partners with whom one takes on the world in the form of a challenge, whether it is getting around the ring at a collected canter or a ten-day trip into the wilderness. A psychologist who has studied bereavement in those who have lost horses calls it a symbiotic "partnership relationship" that is marked by "mutual trust, intuitive understanding, and task-oriented alliance." Engaging in competition causes all of these aspects to speed up, compress, and intensify. In the words of one endurance competitor, "When you spend so much time conditioning and preparing for a ride, you cannot believe the bond you develop with your horse. [My dangerously unridable Arabian] Tom went from outlaw to trusted partner." It is almost, some say, that you learn to read each other's minds. Interestingly, the only other time in life that happens is when Mommy picks us up and holds us close because she knows exactly what we want even though we have no words to say it. I make no claims about this, just point it out. I just point out that it feels very much like bliss.

IT IS ALSO, bizarrely enough, a happy thing to be in so much danger. No one really talks about it; it is apparently not central to the experience in the way it is with skydiving or driving a race car. But it is undeniably true, with the American Medical Association reporting that equestrian-related accidents cause the most common sports injuries seen in emergency rooms; every eight minutes, in fact, a rider is hurt badly enough to require a doctor. And 90 percent of those injured are female. This no doubt merely reflects the current level of participation of girls and women, not their abilities, or even a reversal of the conditions that caused S. Sidney to write in his popular late-nineteenth-century *The Book of the Horse:*

> Not to put too fine a point upon it, the majority of horse-women . . . ride abominably; so badly that it must be presumed, looking at the rarity of accidents, that they enjoy

the benefit of the special providence said to preside over
the lives of idiots and drunkards.

Now, no such providence looks out for women, perhaps as part of
the exchange that allowed them to compete, unprecedentedly, on
literally the same field as men. The clippings fall like autumn leaves
from my folder: a three-day-eventer, Amanda Pirie Warrington,
killed not so long ago at age twenty-nine at a trials in Maryland;
twenty-eight-year-old steeplechase jockey Bitsy Patterson put into
a coma after tipping over a fence while going after the Marion du
Pont Scott Colonial Cup; British rider Polly Phillips done in on
the cross-country course of the Scottish open championships,
becoming the third fatality among British eventers in 1999; the
American Julie Krone, called "the winningest" female jockey ever,
announces her retirement from the track after coping with so
many horrific injuries (such smashups as a shattered ankle that also
caused her to be caught full in the chest by another running horse
and flipped over, and another one resulting in two broken hands)
that the flashbacks finally eclipsed her confidence to go on. I see,
too, that not only stars engaged in major-league competition have
trouble; it is something that comes to find you in the backyard on
a sunny day. Read about the sixty-two-year-old from Virginia
horse country who was temporarily paralyzed from the neck
down when a pony kicked her. Sixteen months later she was riding again, although she fell off and broke her leg a few years later.
(She says this, too, will not deter her from riding again.) Another
item: "Rider Crushed by Horse in Park." The vice-president of the
World Sidesaddle Federation, Marti Friddle, writes of an example
of this kind of accident, the one that is so unexpected it ought to
be utterly expected.

> This horse was nearly bomb-proof. . . . We were cantering
> during a lesson in a big ring with a board fence, just cruis-
> ing along. Between one stride and the next I suddenly had
> no horse under the front end—he went down on his chin
> and somersaulted in the air behind me. I was thrown for-

ward into the fence, because we were in a corner. Just knowing that horse was tumbling behind me was enough to send me scrambling up those boards for dear life. . . . I got out of that wreck with only minor splinters in my hands from climbing the fence, but it taught me a valuable lesson: You can get hurt in even the most benign circumstances.

Indeed. Here is another bit, about a young woman who now has a new heart courtesy of a forty-year-old who died after being thrown from a horse. Naturally, she has become dauntless, and at the age of thirty-six used her kind gift to climb one of the highest mountains in the United States.

THE IDEA THAT women need to be protected and are somehow the weaker sex is so bizarre that once again only classical projection could explain it: Men, knowing *they* might well be the weaker ones but unable to accept the knowledge consciously, pin it outside themselves as if that will make it true. Some women find themselves longing for the impossible to become possible in the form of an experiment whereby men could be tested for their ability to withstand childbirth; they think they know what the results would be, given the alacrity with which so many men hop into bed on first getting the sniffles and begin moaning about their terrible illness. Absolutely nothing in actual experience points to any greater weakness on the part of females, but the idea has become so institutionalized that women, at least in the United States, are still prohibited from participating fully in some of the last activities to remain sacred solely to men: active combat and football.

Not that women haven't tried, numerous times and on both counts. One of the more interesting attempts was actually conceived by a man, a British sergeant-major who had been wounded in the Sudan in 1898. He reasoned that mounted nurses would be able to arrive faster on the scene than either the pedestrian stretcher-bearers or the horse-drawn ambulances. In London in

1907 he began to put his plan into action, finding no small number of women enthusiastic to undertake training in first aid, riding (including some cavalry drill), signaling, and camp routine. They would be in the advance guard, so that if they themselves survived the attack, they would be ready to tend the wounded immediately. Their equestrian training was overseen by The Blues, who discovered that many of "the girls" were already accomplished from many seasons on the hunt field. Despite their willingness and their skill, however, the women of the First Aid Nursing Yeomanry were to find that their biggest battle would be fought against the men at home. One group of members having lunch in a Brighton restaurant were forced to sit at a screened-off table and to be escorted out a back entrance. Others found themselves booed in the streets, or even attacked by rock throwers who took them for suffragettes.

They were thanked by being turned down for service in 1914.

TO ME, ONE of the most admirable things about both Dominique and Amelia is their fearlessness. It is something I always admire in anyone who displays it, and I have gotten pretty good at scenting out the real thing from the bluff, though nowhere near as good as any horse or dog. Neither of these women need to pretend, because it is as much part of them as their blood or bones. But since they are made of the aforementioned perishables, they are not entirely untouchable.

The sound of hammering filled the barn when I entered one morning. Stuart was in one of the empty stalls, attaching heavy wire mesh across the window and all the open bars. It looked as though they were expecting a tiger. Instead, Stuart informed me, Dom was getting a new job: a Lipizzan stallion who had, the story went, tried to kill his owner, rearing up to knock her down and trying to dismember her under his hooves. (So much for the magical bond between women and their horses.) The owner didn't want to geld, and she didn't want to sell; she wanted Dominique to find out what was wrong and to train him to be the kind of equine who could live with others. Dominique, I am sure, said, "Sure." At first she gave him as a project to Amelia, who could soon be found in his stall speaking quietly to him as she groomed him, or walking him around on a lead line, or longeing him in the arena. Before long I was going into his stall, too, just as if he were any other horse, to pick out the manure or change the water in his buckets. I would keep up a stream of soothing chatter as much to calm my nerves as his, though he never offered me the supreme compliment, the one that always filled me with private joy—the spontaneous act of resting the full weight of the chin on my shoulder near the neck.

Soon the wire mesh was taken down. Dominique consulted an equine massage therapist to see if pain was the source of his bad mood, and even a psychic who claimed to be able to read horses' minds over the telephone. Yes, it seems there's some pain on this side of his neck; yes, he seems to have trouble tracking to the right. The work and the consultations continued.

Then one day Dominique went into his stall to change the water in the buckets; when things needed doing and there was no one else around to do them, as was often the case, it fell to her. And as she turned from her innocent task she suddenly found herself halfway up the wall of the stall with three feet of air beneath her. The stallion had the flesh of her upper left arm between his teeth.

Over the next days and weeks the wound took on different forms and colors, expanding, blowing up, pulling back and shriveling the skin as if it had been burned. It had been an almost mystical experience for Dominique; she said she saw madness overtake his eyes, which was just as suddenly replaced with cognizance. That was when he opened his jaw and she dropped back to earth once more. It is not normal, she tells me, for horses to release by opening up; they release by biting through.

Whether or not he had regained his senses from a journey into insanity, Dominique would no longer work with him. She wouldn't go into his stall, and she wouldn't lead him out to the paddocks. A few months later, he was gone.

20

WAR

I USED TO LOVE TO POKE around in the basement, for all that the air down there was almost unbreathable with mildew. That's because the source of that mildew, my mother's old magazines, was what I was in part after. They were stacked on shelves, the years' worth of *New Yorkers*, *Vogues*, *House & Gardens*. They were of a commanding scale then, calling for nothing less than allegiance, none of today's penny-pinching, eight-by-ten, throwaway mien. And in them I found a map to where I wanted to go, by way of where I had been: an attempt to divine the mysteries of why my mother was as magnificent, as beautiful, as godly, as she was to me. The women in their satin shirtwaists and spike heels; the deep azures and emeralds of the clothes, the drinks, the pools, the gardens at dusk; all represented the place and the person I wanted to inhabit and become, and they were so intoxicating to me I wanted to fall into the photos and drown.

The years combed the passion into a somewhat neater arrangement. I just wanted to look a little bit like those women who were in such unquestioning command of themselves, their makeup brushes, and their fears. My mother gave me a subscription to *Vogue,* renewed every Christmas with a discreet white envelope placed in the boughs of the tree. I was continuing the line, participating in not only a matriarchal but a cultural tradition. Did I know the pictures were only as deep as the pages they were printed on? Face value: Take the beauty at face value.

HERE IS ANOTHER story about what is hidden.

It is said that in the East, in Japan and China and elsewhere, menopause is not a medical emergency. Women do not seek help for hot flashes or fear that their bones will soon be looking like sponge. Women do not see advertisements in magazines picturing smiling models of a certain age picking daisies in a field without a care in the world, causing them to think that since they currently have more than one care, they must need a prescription for the medication the ad sells.

In the United States, more than nine million women—soon to balloon as the post–World War II population bubble reaches the time for its "change of life"—have sought succor from a pill that promises them so much. (Our preternatural fondness for pills goes without remarking even if I remark on it now, so to remind you that our revered doctors also like them for their own reasons. So do the pharmaceutical companies, who find that just by promising things that people want so desperately that it doesn't even matter that no pill can really deliver them, they can become the Rulers of the Universe, or at least of bodies such as the Food and Drug Administration.) There are other pills, and other means—ask again what is different in Japan—but one pill above all others has found much favor.

Here is the gift of the female horse. She stands in what is known as the pee line, along with tens of thousands of others of her kind. It is good that she is part draft, of the breeds known for their stoic patience, since nothing was ever so needed. She is pregnant, and she can barely move. The ground under her feet is concrete, and the straw that covers it is not cleaned as often as it might be. She lips the automatic waterer, hoping that it will come on again and deliver some water soon, for she is very thirsty. But that does not happen, because of something to do with the black tubing that is arranged around her hindquarters, and that chafes her between the legs. Her urine never reaches the ground.

She has long ago stopped feeling the vague panic that used to come when she realized she couldn't get out of this stall, that she was trapped in the way that she could never bear, that she couldn't scratch her back against the earth, that she simply couldn't do anything but stand, seemingly unto eternity, stand. So she was unable to appreciate the fact that one day they came and untied her. It was now just another of the things they did. So much time had passed.

Her foal came. Sometimes, more often than seemed quite right, the foal never got up. Sometimes it had crooked legs or hooves that seemed to be made of soft clay. But something would still stir inside the mothers, and most of the foals would be licked all over and nudged up to life. And just when the grass was tasting good, the sun shining, a large double-decker truck pulled up the drive. The mothers could hear the foals calling out—would the teller anthropomorphize too much to call the sound desperate, afraid? Later, at the other place, the foals would mill about, instinct forcing them toward futility in the form of empty teats of one another. But just for a short while.

THE PILL IS KNOWN the world over by several names: Premarin, Prempro, Premphase, Prempak C, Premique, Premelle. It is the most widely prescribed drug in America, and by far the most popular estrogen-replacement therapy (diet change and exercise not being very popular at all). Most women who take it do not know where it comes from, because the drug's maker does not tell them, not even in all that small print that takes up an entire page of the ad in magazines, and the magazines do not tell them, not even in articles that go on and on about what the doctors say about estrogen. And the doctors do not tell them, for their own reasons. But the funny thing is that they hid the truth in plain sight: Pre(gnant)mar(e)(ur)in. It was clever, because so few would think to look there.

Or care. That must be it.

THE EDITOR OF *VOGUE* comes from England; she is the embodiment of the woman in command of herself. She is very, very thin, to show that she is in charge of the food she eats, not the other way around. She wears her hair in a Louise Brooks bob, to show that the years cannot dictate to her. And when some very bad, very silly people, who did not like the fact that her magazine shows pictures of deluxe models shouting "Let them eat cake!" as they pull their soft animal skins about them, vilely interrupted her very sparse lunch by throwing a dead something or other right on her plate, we might imagine she knew just how to get back at them. She knew that her pages already sold millions of tubs and tubes of colors that previously killed some small things in cages when they were painted onto their eyes or their skin, but she could do more. There would be more pictures of soft animal skins, with bigger headlines and better pictures, to capture the glamour of the monkey-fur trim and make every woman want to own it just to show how insouciantly they could pretend it was not even there. There would be items about the wonderful fabric everyone wanted, and royalty had: It was called shah-tush, and the reason it was so rare was because the wild goats in Pakistan who caused it to be so unbelievably soft would die when they were captured and shorn, and they were thus getting rarer by the moment, which made shah-tush even more darling, if illegal; slyly mention that it is "reportedly" prohibited for import but go no further, and she knew that half her readers would not stop until they had gotten some shah-tush for themselves.

She could declare that Pony Skin Is for Spring—and indeed it would be the spring for pony skin. Then she could enlist the help of her food writer, because he was already the kind of man who liked to drink deeply of everything he wanted to drink of, to suck the marrow out of life's very bones literally as well as metaphorically. He would instruct the readership in the finer points of French fries—or rather, pardon, *frites*—and deliver to them the solemn news that the only fries worth having, at least if you wanted to live the kind of life the *Vogue* reader so dearly wants to live, are fried in horse fat. (He would publish in another magazine the definitive word on the dangerous inferiority of vegetable matter as food, under the title "Salad: The Silent Killer.")

The editor knows that the only sound that really counts in this world is the simple ringing of "I want," and to make her readers whisper it with every page they turn has become her art, even to make them feel want so keenly that the desire to own these things whatever their cost soon feels inseparable from the desire to live a life full of joy and happiness.

Now they smile so beguilingly, and move with grace. Their hearts are full, knowing they walk in beauty. Their perfume masks the faint odor of death that oddly seems to rise from the ground.

21

THE END

WE HAVE SET OURSELVES above all. The animals *with* whom we came into being are now all *underneath* us. The one species that has no controls on its own population has put itself to the task of controlling the numbers of every other species. (Of course, mistakes do occasionally occur; it's only human. And so we currently have to dispose of some twenty million dogs and cats in this country every year. At least they do not all go to waste! Some have a second glorious coming in the promisingly colorful pencils and jars that help make a woman look her best.) We prefer not to know what happens before and after, just that the surplus is gone, removed quietly in the night like our garbage, and disappeared—a verb used most aptly in the case of those enemies of a military regime who vanish suddenly without being heard from again; its usage here may offend, but really, what could be more appropriate when this human junta will brook no opposition, offer no recourse, to the finality of its condemnations? Meanwhile, the memorials are eloquent in their way, if you know where to look: the cans of lubricant, the bottles of shampoo, the boxes of Jell-O and jars of pills, all stand in their silent rows, ready to bear their testimony and to make the cupboards of our homes an appropriately poignant cemetery for these unknown millions dead.

We are happiest not knowing. Just don't tell me anything, please. It will ruin my day.

Like the Web site for the equine sanctuary that warns visitors with weak stomachs to go no farther lest they see, by way of some video footage, what really goes on in a horse slaughterhouse, there is a warning here. Do not proceed if you prefer not to know what happened to your reining horse after he progressed through three owners, finally to come up lame as the possession of someone who really needed to recoup some money if this was going to be it; or what happened in September to the ponies adored all summer long by the girls at camp (*Oh, my Esmeralda . . .*); or where the Amish's buggy horses find themselves when there is no more to be gotten out of them by those gentle, frugal people; or where all manner of damaged show horses, racehorses, backyard horses, wild horses, hack stable horses, urban carriage horses, Premarin horses, old horses, go when they go to their end. We wouldn't eat our friends—the thought appalls us, discomfits us, disturbs us—but we don't mind if others do, just as long as they stay on their foreign shores. This airplane you're on—why, right now its lightly humming hold beneath your feet may be whisking away the refrigerated remains of our most noble and exalted companion. Order your cocktail.

THIS IS WHAT THE end looks like. Up to thirty-six hours in a trailer without food, water, or exercise. Confusion, untended injury, fear. Electric prods toward a trip through a chute from which escape is impossible but frequently tried; at some point, realization—uncanny, onlookers agree, how you know, absolutely, that they know. A bolt in the head. Maybe another, or two or three. A chain around a hind fetlock, then *up*—hanging by one leg, still alive technically, but soon bled to finality. The only way to become safe for the dinner plate.

All five equine slaughterhouses (the number fluctuates) in the United States are owned by Belgians. Beltex, in Fort Worth, Texas, kills four hundred to five hundred horses a week; nationwide, the yearly number runs between one hundred thousand and two hundred thousand. Some of them are the vaunted symbols of this great land and its greatest attribute, the wild horses of the West. They will be dinner for some Belgians, some French, perhaps some Japanese, occasionally some Mexicans.

> I have some serious concerns that some of the oldest herds with the real true ancestral blood have already been flushed down somebody's toilet in Europe. . . . The colts often are not worth anything because they are so small. So they usually would just knock them in the head and throw them in the gut wagon. . . . A mare might be just about due to foal and it didn't matter. Went through the plant and they just cut her open and throw it in the gut wagon. . . . [A] real difficult thing for me to talk about was the time I was in the building and I happened to look down because I heard a big ruckus in the chutes. . . . There was this black wild stallion that they were trying to get up the chute. But he was real smart. He knew what was coming. And he reared. He turned around and tried to crawl over the top of the other horses to get back down the chute. . . . So they got all the crew out there. And they used the electric prods on him to prod him up. They used ropes around his neck to jerk him up. And they did everything they could. They finally got him into the chute where they could use a stun gun, which is just a bullet that goes

straight down into the top of the head. . . . And finally the guy on the kill floor came up, running upstairs, laughing. And he says, "You know that son of a bitch just didn't want to die." He said, "But we got him. He got loose on the kill floor after six shots and they had to take a rifle before they could finally kill him." And when he said that, it made me so sad to think that that kind of spirit is what we kill every day and we don't even think about it.

—Spoken by an anonymous "killer buyer"
(slaughterhouse broker), in *The Last Wild Horses*, 1995

We decide who lives and who dies. The worthless die.

One of the great pleasures of reading animal stories is the consistency of their implicit answers to an implicit question: So who really is smarter, man or horse? The tales of rescued horses—a cheap title for a collection of them would be "Nags to Riches"—are extreme in this regard.

Margaret Cabell Self writes of the story of Sky Rocket, whom she met as a sore-ridden near-skeleton one step from the abattoir. Something in his eyes—"the look of eagles"—caused her to give him a try. She mounted and discovered that although he was weak with starvation, he moved well and had quite an affinity for jumping, even if, upon landing from his first one, he did go immediately to his knees. She bought him for fifty dollars (his valuation as a ten-dollar carcass had quickly risen) and he regained his health in her care. That's when he demonstrated his love of jumping just for the pleasure of it, spending days jumping out of and back into his paddock. He was shown at Madison Square Garden and won two blues; if he had been a bit taller, Self believed, he would have gone to the Olympics.

Another such story comes from Vian Smith, the British journalist who recounted his lifetime experiences with horses in the previously mentioned and uncommonly lovely reminiscence *Horses in the Green Valley*. He tells of how his children came home with a sack of bones from the local pony fair, at which semiwild

Dartmoor ponies were dispatched to new homes as well as to dog-food canneries. They gave her a pasture and left her to decide for herself whether she wanted to trust humans anymore. After a slow process, she learned that the best treats were found inside the house, especially when the family was eating. Cheese became a favorite. Inside, she also ascertained, was where one could watch a rousing western on TV, and upon discovering the excitement of all those horses clappity-clapping across the little screen, she could always be found planted in front of it. Her every day, it seemed, existed as a rebuke to the appalling hubris of humans.

It makes you want to collect enough stories so that finally you can have a fistful of proof to wave in the face of the doubters. The Godolphin Arabian, one of the foundation sires of the mighty Thoroughbred breed, was earlier thought fit only to pull a Paris water cart.

In 1919 horseman Freddie Bontecu traveled from New York to Ontario on a buying trip. He already had his carload when he spotted a forlorn gray three-year-old shivering in the field; it was ten degrees below zero. He felt sorry and bought the youngster for one hundred dollars. The youngster turned into Ballymacshane, a jumper who won his owner more than twenty-five thousand dollars and led all horses in winnings at American horse shows for five years.

Snow Man was the name given to a plow horse who was bought off the knackers' truck for seventy dollars in 1956. Two years later he was jumping victoriously at some of the country's most important shows, and his owner reportedly turned down an offer of four hundred thousand dollars for him.

Craansford, in the fifties one of the Royal greys—Her Majesty the queen's personal carriage horses, who cannot be harnessed except by her command—began life pulling an Irish farm cart.

A 16.1-hand Thoroughbred weighing 850 pounds and suffering from severe hoof punctures and abscesses from being ridden unshod caught the eye of a trainer who bought him in 1992 at the meat price of $450. After four months of intensive rehabilitation, his new owner was able to discover that he had a definite talent: dressage. He won the First Level Connecticut Freestyle Championship, and has now gone on to school Second Level.

The worthless die.

22

BRIDGE

S O IT *IS* TRUE you are a somewhat neglectful memoirist, the interviewer asks me with a touch of concocted drama in his voice. He has noticed, hovering in the air a bit like a moth that seems to be a butterfly, another memory from very early times, when all along I professed there were none. (But that is what this whole thing is about, I would like to say in my defense—being led to find the false back to the closet behind which the *real* goods are stored.) It may be a bit faulty around the edges, though, so caveat emptor. But it is nonetheless true that I would spend what seemed like hours at a time rocking back and forth—at what may be called a frenzied pace—on the plastic horse (bay, inside of nostrils and tongue bright red, fervid look in the eyes) suspended on four great silver springs that went *creak, creak, creak, creak.* I would often do this in the silent but pleasant company of our twice-weekly maid, Julia, as she did the ironing. I do not know where my mother was. It seemed that she showed herself only when she determined it was time for me to remove the only outfit I would wear, day in and day out, a cowboy getup replete with little maroon and black boots. Occasionally this item of clothing needed to be washed, my mother would try to explain, while I would scream and run out the back door in an approximation of someone who is being chased by the determined population of a burst hornets' nest.

Thus the hobbyhorse, endlessly rocking, that I rode until it never got tired. Unlike the one I ride today, a less forgiving beast.

23

WE ARE/ARE NOT

I T IS EARLY DECEMBER and I am at the therapeutic riding center. I know a session is to begin soon, but I have not
been apprised of the nature of the patients. Will they be
blind? paralyzed? addicted? I wait for their arrival in the cold barn,
taking off my gloves to warm my hands against the live heat of a
horse who is being tacked up in preparation.

Soon they are here. Six boys have come running in, followed
by a teacherly voice: "Now, remember what we learned about
running around horses. I *said,* Steven, stop it!" Giggles and shared
looks amounting to the child's credo: I heard you and will submit
but do not ask me to acknowledge that I did.

I am looking hard, trying to find something. Some disability; where is it? These six- and seven-year-olds are about as normal as you can get, some quiet, some shy, some downright brats. These particular children look less in need of help than the horses, living in standing stalls with abused saddles pinned to their backs for much of the day; mainly elderly, they still must work seven days a week. The boys evince little interest in the animals themselves, except to shout, "Oh, not *Snowy!* I don't like *him!*" Finally I have to ask one of the volunteers what it is these children need therapy for. Attention Deficit Disorder, I am told. Riding is supposed to help them learn to focus. That seems to beg a question, especially as these days the questions are as thick as ants on watermelon sugar. If the problem were truly chemical in origin, how could a nonchemical intervention affect it (and conversely, if behavior modification works, why resort to medications that have never been tested for long-term effects?). Clearly I do not understand something, and the boys merely appear as unfocused as every child their age had ever been and ever would be; it is involuntary when I avert my eyes halfway through as they are asked to stop their horses and an adult comes around to each of them to offer their morning dose of little pills. The boys focus intently on the benevolent hand reaching up to give them the medicine that will make them well.

Then they continue their lesson, under the eye of their professionally chipper but personally sour tutor, who berates them constantly and views their only problem, if her attitude is any guide, as willfulness. At one point an altercation between two horses threatens to become serious, and it occurs to me that perhaps the horses know something about the true condition of their riders, given what I had heard of their unflagging protection of the genuinely weak or needy. At any rate, the woman running the class blames the two boys for the near incident, though an observer might as easily have faulted her for allowing it to happen on her watch, because she wasn't watching quite carefully enough.

When it comes time to dismount, one little boy is having

trouble keeping his horse from prematurely leaving the ring, and as there is a dearth of volunteers, I go over to assist with the reins. As we then stand waiting for further orders, one of the horses unsheaths his impressive equipment to pitch a line of steaming yellow froth into the sand. A few of the boys find the sight riveting and hilarious at once; there are cries and pointings and hands over eyes. *"Gross!"* they cry one after another. I mention to one boy that his penis does pretty much the same sort of thing, and that horse and boy had both received one to aid in purely animal functions. He literally stomps his little foot. "I am *not* an animal!" he protests, and suddenly a school-yard bitchiness rises in me as I respond, "You are too an animal," now fully prepared to engage in "am not," "are too," until I should pin him flat on his back on the turf. No one had ever told this little creature, this little sufferer, the most basic fact about his existence. He was growing up not knowing what he was.

WHAT IS THE SOURCE of my infantile petulance in this matter? Why does what I see with my eyes differ from what others see with theirs? What has happened to me in the quarter-century since that bon voyage dinner, or the thirty-five years since I borrowed *Charlotte's Web* from the Highland Square library? Why is it that I now see no innocently unimportant sign at the New London ferry—NO ANIMALS IN THIS AREA—but instead an instruction in a dangerous irony, since there are human animals lounging all around it? It's as if I have noticed a small inch-long crack in a mile of sidewalk, and on closer inspection see that there is some sort of water flowing underneath it, no, a river, and it has banks and trees and occasional cities and barges and factories, but meanwhile people hurry past my kneeling form with their eyes straight ahead. I feel flabbergasted and sickened and angered and despairing and amazed: No one *cares* that a whole other world exists beneath our feet! Hello, hello, I call in a faintly echoing voice that seems now to be disappearing into that miniature crevasse, and I sit down in perplexity and try to think.

It must have something to do with some first little denial,

some tiny misstatement. *We are not animals.* But such a small thing to pay attention to, when there are so many great lies afoot—read the paper, watch the news!—and trembling masses of people cringing before their blows.

But, oh, how we do not want to be animals. (And the girls who become horses . . . ?) We keep insisting we are not, as if the repetition—man *and* animal, man *and* animal—will make it true. I find a parallel in the less meaningful but no less inscrutable shopping list my mother once made out that has now passed into family lore: She requested that someone go to the store and purchase "fruits and pears." We do not want to be animals, yet we have tongue, teeth, ear, liver, and so do they. What logic would then give only us the ability to feel, to love, to need, to communicate, and to think? Moreover, those who have seen one say that an autopsy will cure you of believing there's any substantive difference between us and a raw leg of lamb. Yet in the absence of any compelling evidence that we are not animals, we invent some. We call into service the finest, most ingenious flower of our creativity. Morality, the soul: perfectly constructed to be impossible to prove to exist, equally hard to refute. Still, the basis on which so much death and pain is founded, sentence pronounced without fair trial. (Descartes nailed down the howling family dog and took him apart like a clock.)

But as I sit, all I see with my newly strange eyes are good little animals on two legs, with basic needs, spending little lives trying to get them met. As I contemplate the shifting plates of this terribly strange world, at this moment, another animal stirs within me, waiting to be born. No one will consider it right to take him to discover for his or her own edification how he might react to being deprived of any warmth or love, or how long (days? weeks? let's carefully mark it down in our records) it will take him to die from stove cleaner injected into his veins, or what he would look like in a cage with an instructive placard placed before it. Still, the fact is that he will have no language, no powers of reasoning. His worldly status to the ethicist studying his case will look identical to that of the veal calf or the Pentagon's test beagle but for one thing. No, not that he is human and they are not, for what right is conferred by that? It is simply that they *can;* they can do what they do to them, and I won't let them do those things to him. The ethical construct we have chosen as our paramount guide—"Might makes right"—contains an inherent and awful sarcasm, and the sound of it is appalling. So we have decided simply not to say it.

In the case of my own tender and helpless infant, the books instruct me to pay attention to his needs, to fulfill them on demand; thus will trust be created. Ignore them, frustrate them, and something dangerous, like hollow ground, will be installed permanently in the center of his being. He will come to look like those criminals in court, staring straight ahead as the litany of their unimaginable cruelties is read while the families of the victims look in vain for some remorse, some sense that the criminals understand what they have done; in its absence they proclaim the presence of evil. But if the milk comes when it is wanted, it feeds the sense of right and wrong: I want, and it is right that you should give it to me. And surely, if he were never to experience giving, how would he know how to give?

Those who are well provided for grow up naturally to feel in their milk-fed bones that the society around them takes care of things; it *cares.* Those who were denied the things their animal hearts cried out for—justice, understanding, sympathy, strong arms that cradle in love—feel that they are not a part of anything good. They were trained as precisely as any foot soldier that they must get their needs met any way they can. They will, too. And at last the prisons open their arms to them.

This is what we are. Needs. Our conception of the universe flows outward from the region of our large intestines.

"WE TEND TO SUPPRESS [the knowledge that fear is a universal emotion in the animal kingdom] from our consciousness, perhaps because we need to preserve 'nature' as an area of innocence to which we can withdraw when discontented with people," wrote Yi-Fu Tuan in *Landscapes of Fear,* a scrupulous exploration of how those ur-human attributes, from religiosity to cultural beliefs of all stripes, are a response to that ur-animal attribute, fear.

We tend to suppress the knowledge that we are in any way just like them, or else some terribly unsavory details of the lives we have so carefully constructed will be revealed, and we will see that we have put our bricks together with very cheap mortar.

The suppression can reach almost comical heights, so long as you have a peculiar sense of humor. This is where I appreciate *The New York Times* most. (You may find your morning paper equally diverting.) Every other week there is a breathless report about the latest research indicating—*gadzooks!*—that animals have been discovered to have a *rudimentary language!* (An American without Spanish tends to feel the same about Spaniards.) Chimpanzees possess culture, teaching different things to one another depending on their geographic milieu! (Whereupon some Einstein writes an indignant letter to the editor protesting that chimpanzees have produced no Mozart.) Humans have been discovered to attract one another with mysterious scents known as pheromones! (When all along, what, we thought we found our mating partners through a tough and impartial judicial process?) Then I turn the page to find a half-page piece on the increasing prevalence of factory hog farms, in which I read about money, farmers, smells, places, opinions, jokes, prognostications, and down and down the columns until my eyes are going as fast as it is possible to read without turning type into blur. It ends with a *thunk* and I sit there, incredulous. There is nothing, no single small word, about the *hogs themselves.* The creatures with whom we share tongue, teeth, ear, liver, as well as the urge to feed soft pink newborns with milk. The creatures whom we consign, twenty-five in a lot, to life in a pen that is twenty feet by nine feet. The creatures who are so like us we are afraid to see it, that we may see what we have become.

I SIT AND PUZZLE over the anger and hatred that is directed to those who see and speak out about the perpetuation of sadism, unconcern, and lavish denial in our various systems—food, fashion, cosmetics, weapons, medicines. The favorite epithet shot at them like arrows is "extremists," and we know where *they* belong. As if it is possible to care too much about the pain of others, any others, who are capable of feeling it. So here's a notion to try on for size: civil rights extremists.

As I sit a memory comes to me of the first time I came across the derisively used term "animal rightists" in a horse magazine; I blanch now at the naïveté that caused me to feel shock when I realized that just because someone loves horses, she does not necessarily love animals. Animal rightists are, in fact, the enemies of certain horse lovers, those who love horses as some people love steak.

There is a woman who has devoted much of her adult life to saving horses and other hooved animals from the abuse and horror that is often visited upon them, simply because it can be; she sends out fundraising mailings with pictures on them that freeze the blood of anyone with half a conscience. But she has things clear in her mind: These and no others get saved. She is careful to go on the record as being a realist, no extremist she.

This is the same stance maintained by some other women I know of who have devoted themselves to equine welfare. But in their case it is a ruse. Because they know that nothing would queer their reputations, everything they stand for, as much as being known to be . . . vegetarians. Their cause is so sacred that they would even eat a steak in public to vouch for their credentials as sane human beings, the kind who know where to draw the line in the sand of their compassion.

YOU SEE, I AM afraid, too. It is not that I am not certain about what I see through the crack in the sidewalk. It is that I am afraid of despair, of that sinking feeling in which I am falling, falling through the dark, alone, and anticipating the crash at the end even as I fear it will never come. And the despair comes every day, with every day's new evidence of the sheer spread of our enterprise of cruelty, and the obdurance of our silence about it. Many years ago the halls of public opinion were ringing with denunciations of vivisection, made by men and women of great stature and sense— John Ruskin and Abraham Lincoln, Queen Victoria and Albert Schweitzer, Mark Twain and George Bernard Shaw ("The distinction is not between useful and useless experiments, but between barbarous and civilized behaviour. Vivisection is a social evil because if it advances human knowledge, it does so at the expense of human character."). But now that vivisection has been institutionalized at a level that would have caused these elders to take up arms, their equivalents today are speechless on the subject. I sit and puzzle over why the good and kind people around me cannot hear the sounds of millions upon millions of their kin tortured to death; surely they know? Then, why do they not pause? I am reminded of something I heard on the radio the other day, a man speaking about the shameful days of open segregation: "Remember," he said, "the majority *can* be wrong."

And I am afraid of the vehemence of their hatred and contempt for those whose ears and eyes are such unhappy witnesses. Not because I do not understand it, but because I do. I believe it has something to do with Konrad Lorenz's observation that in the world of animals—in our world—"the most violent form of fighting behavior is motivated by fear." We are afraid of our fear. It would be so frightening to acknowledge that we are just like our quiet victims.

And so, to keep them different, that we may in good conscience continue to use them for our myriad ends, we employ one of two approaches. Caution: They only *seem* opposed. The most common could be termed, after the psychoanalysts' joke, the Elephant in the Room: the steadfast denial that something so huge even exists, in this case the ever more monumental infrastructure of death that forms the little-visited basement on top of which we have built society. (Thus can Junior—tears in his eyes and passion in his heart—watch *Babe* again and again, with its Orwellian opening scene in a factory farm and its implicit condemnation of human disregard for animal life, and then be led unprotestingly to table to eat his meal of meat.) The other is best-sellingly popular of late: the religious belief in a miraculous and "spiritual" bond between animals and people, in which animals appear in dreams, communicate with the dead, know to save us from falling over the brink of a catastrophe unseen by us. A very pretty aggrandizement, yes, but insensible to the obvious: Of course we can relate, deeply or otherwise, with animals—we *are* animals, just another brand, or like Gorgonzola to their Cheddar. To make it such a mystical event forces them back onto their side of the wall, where they have long been forced to huddle, waiting for us to understand.

I SIT WITH a book in my lap, four-hundred-plus pages of schol-arly articles collected in *Cruelty to Animals and Interpersonal Violence,* and it is illuminating if not entertaining reading. The title has already made me wonder that if we are not animals, how could a desire to inflict pain on them be so consistently associated by psy-chologists with the desire to inflict pain on humans? ("I am *not* an animal!") Burning the family pet or breaking the necks of the neighbor's rabbits is now considered the training wheels on a future serial killer's bike.

There is much fodder here for the theory that a little lie can beget a world of larger ones. I begin reading a 1988 study by Temple Grandin that looked at "Behavior of Slaughter Plant and Auction Employees Toward the Animals," and I find I am losing some of my former squeamishness because I have recently decid-ed that if I cannot look the truth in the face, then I am no better than those who deny it. My new attitude causes rough going, however, because the pictures I look at make me lose sleep some nights, and torn bits of anecdote come into my head at untoward times during the day, and I feel an urge to unburden myself of them, but I know it is unfair to haunt others as well with, for instance, the image that keeps returning to me of the pregnant dog whose unborn puppies were cut from her belly. She tried desper-ately in that moment to lick them with her tongue—the scientists fascinated to note that the instinct to care for her young went undiminished by the restraining nails in her paws—as they were pulled forever away.

The abstract of this paper informs me that "Abuses of animals at auctions and slaughter plants occur often. Commonly observed abuses include the dragging of crippled animals, hitting, and excessive prodding." A "disturbing finding" was that half the markets rated as having cruel handling allowed young children to abuse animals, hitting pigs on the nose, slamming cattle with boards, tormenting calves with electric prods; no adult was observed to make an effort to stop them. The author cites one slaughter-plant employee, particularly cruel to the cows, who later revealed that he had been forced to kill a pet steer when he was a child, whereupon he "could never love another beef again." Here is one boy who was denied the justice his animal heart cried out for, all right.

The most common management psychology, the study found, was denial. The word *killing* is not used, replaced instead by *dispatching* or *processing* (and having as analogue the shiny cold bricks of beef in the supermarket that thankfully for most look nothing like a portion of corpse). The people whose actual job it is to "process" the animals had to come up with more creative methods. A previous study had found that "permeating most responses was the theme of protecting oneself from the full impact of the act by isolating one's feelings from the act." More common is "the mechanical approach," in which the employee manages to have no feelings whatsoever, and so can "chitchat about the weather and gossip while they kill hundreds of animals per day." This desensitization is by no means immediate, however, since these employees reported that they were initially greatly disturbed by the act.

Another approach is the sadistic one, in which employees go out of their way to inflict pain on the animals they are about to kill, justifying their actions by saying "They are just animals anyway" (familiar words to most soldiers and any genocidal dictator). "By devaluing the animal," the author states, "the person justifies in his mind the cruel things he does to it."

The paper at this point cites the famous experiments of the sixties and early seventies in which seemingly average people were turned into "torturers" within a short amount of time by following the apparent behest of their scientist leaders; they were told they would have to administer electrical shocks starting at fifteen volts and moving up by fifteen volts to a subject if he made mistakes on a learning task. They were shown levers marked "Danger: Severe Shock" as well as the even more ominous marking of "XXX." Knowing this, they went full ahead. ("Custom will reconcile people to any atrocity," Shaw also observed.) Erich Fromm, considering this and a similar experiment, concluded that those who *experienced no conflict* about pushing the button—some, naturally, were a little nervous—had a predisposition to sadism. This was true of a significant share of the sample, about a third of those tested.

The last line of the article, following suggestions for slowing down the increasingly fast rate of slaughter demanded of workers that in turn causes them to be less humane, shakes my resolve to be unshakable. It's that word *paradox,* which is something I look for in art but would prefer be left out of world economy. "The paradox is that it is difficult to care about animals but be involved in killing them." Thus are we all sadists by proxy, every one of us involved in killing them.

I AM STILL SITTING, as night falls, puzzling over the commonly held idea that compassion is a commodity in everpresent danger of running out; that if we direct it toward nonhumans, there won't be any left for us. My friends, even my own blood, have said, "Yes, well, it's terrible, all that suffering, but we must first do something about the people." Yet I have scrutinized the charts and can find no separate chamber in the heart where one might secret away the blood that bleeds for others who do not look just like us. I wonder if these people, seeing a cat with a broken leg lying in the gutter, would pass by with sorrow in their souls and an explanation on their lips: I apologize for not helping you, but you have to understand that it would not be right until all the people have been taken care of, yes?

NOW I HAVE become paralyzed from sitting on the sidewalk and I am unable to stand up. I will molder here, stricken by a fatal dose of perplexity. Before then, though, I hope the mail arrives, and with it the reply to my letter requesting further information. I am sure I am the only person who has ever responded to the deeply forlorn advertisements that have been appearing in *The New York Times Book Review* for years now, placed by a Professor Dr. Hisatoki Komaki of Japan, who broadcasts the fact that he must be a hopeless crank (albeit one with money) with the headline FOUR STEPS TO ABSOLUTE PEACE. When readers get to Goal II—Goal I is "Global disarmament by 2010," ha ha ha—which reads "Total abolition of meat-diet, animal experiments and insecticides," they know they are in the presence of absolute lunacy.

But at least it is not a lonely lunacy. Pythagoras said, in the sixth century B.C., "As long as man continues to be the ruthless destroyer of lower living beings, he will never know health or peace. For as long as men massacre animals, they will kill each other." Dr. Edward Mayhew (1813–1868) followed suit: "What is the use of this fuss about morality when the issue only involves a horse? The first and most difficult teaching of civilization concerns man's behaviour to his inferiors. Make humanity gentle or reasonable toward animals, and strife or injustice between human beings would speedily terminate." The writer Isaac Bashevis Singer was a fervent believer in the connection of brutality to animals and brutality to humans—"as long as human beings will go on shedding the blood of animals, there will never be any peace. There is only one little step from killing animals to creating gas chambers à la Hitler and concentration camps à la Stalin . . . all such deeds are done in the name of 'social justice.' There will be no justice as long as man will stand with a knife or with a gun and destroy those who are weaker than he is"—as was Rachel Carson: "We cannot have peace among men whose hearts find delight in killing any living creature." They were preceded by an early nineteenth-century physician, William Lambe, and by Mohandas Gandhi, and no doubt by many other deranged nitwits, who all believed that the eradication of meat eating would promise the eradication of war.

Man is the animal perhaps most possessed by unbridled curiosity. He has never shied from devising experiments that could only be called bizarre; indeed, some of the oddest have yielded the most enriching knowledge. It seems there is little he will not try. Except this, I think as I am on the verge of losing consciousness and hitting my head on the concrete. Except the one that might deliver his dreams.

Who said Supper?

24

QUEST

ORSES AREN'T VERY SMART. I took it personally every time I heard it, such was the level of my
identification with them, my desire that they be the
most perfect animals on earth. But this wisdom was repeated by
everyone, including those whose whole lives had been spent in
equine company, and the repetition of it was the chisel that drove
it into the rock of truth. And so it seemed to be: Surely an animal
that would act as if a paper bag on the ground were Satan himself
couldn't have that much on the ball. We were smart enough ourselves to see that.

Take the case of Clever Hans, wielded as a potent cautionary tale against the belief that animals can think as well as humans do. This German horse, as everyone knows, captivated turn-of-the-century audiences with his ability to count, tell dates, do mathematics. But the debunkers were hot on his tail. A psychologist finally uncovered the cheap trick that caused a dumb animal to act smart; of course it was a hoax. Hans was reading the subconscious body language of the people around him, who were helpless not to reveal the correct answer when it was proposed in ways so subtle even they were not aware. The deceit Hans had practiced consisted of being able to distinguish head movements as slight as one fifth of a millimeter.

A deceit if you like, but nonetheless an ability that makes knowing how to count or do sums look retarded, to my mind. Not to mention the fact that the insistence on measuring all other species against our own is plain stupid, for arrogance directed solely by egotism is nothing if not the mark of the undeveloped mind. But we may be making some progress, for after centuries of received wisdom, select individuals are now mustering the intelligence that leads to some questioning of that dangerous business. One of the first to try posing her own queries on horses was a British clinical psychologist and horse lover ("my big passion in life, the centre of my childhood") named Moyra Williams; in 1956 she published a study based on observations of her own horses, *Horse Psychology*. She exemplified the true scientific spirit of the youthful inventor who cares nothing for what he has heard all his life and instead needs to know what it feels like to reinvent the wheel for himself. The resulting experiments may be defiantly kooky, but sometimes they radically alter the world. In Moyra Williams's case, it was to do things like load her mare Portia into a train, arm herself with maps, a compass, food, and a mac, and disembark later in the West Country. There she mounted up and dropped the reins. She wanted to see what a horse did when left to her own devices in new territory. Thus she allowed Portia to gallop distractedly back and forth in front of the station, then graze for an entire day, then move off into open country, then spend half the night walking purposefully down a side road in the driving

rain, and finally go out of sight when rest was so desperately needed by Williams that a rather well-used barn "was more welcome
than a five-star hotel." In the morning she set about locating her
horse, employing what she hoped was knowledge she had long
ago gained of Portia's proclivities. At last, "There, sheltering from
the wind, and still sound asleep, were thirty to forty sheep, and
among them, monumental in her beauty, Portia."

It is hard to know at what to be more amazed—the fact that
forty-five years ago it was imaginable to let a horse loose in
Britain, or that Moyra Williams thought to do so in order to let
her horse educate her. But she has a spiritual daughter today in
Evelyn Hanggi, president and co-founder of California's Equine
Research Foundation. There she is investigating horses' ability to
learn and retain knowledge, how they see and reason and respond,
rather than how we have long presumed they see and reason and
respond. Thus much of what she has found contradicts what we
"know," such as there being little communication between the left
and the right sides of the equine brain, the apparent but incorrect
explanation for the fact that the mailbox that posed no danger
whatsoever on the trip out becomes, on the return, a dire threat to
life (the truth is situated in the peculiarities of the horse's unusual
field of vision). She is at last testing horses on their intelligence, not
ours, and naturally all manner of assumptions are finding their
rightful place under tombstones. Her work also calls into question
the way we commonly treat horses, if the basis for it has been
wrong all along. If they are indeed "smart," then what of the steril-
ity of the environments in which we force so many to live? The
stereotypies they devise in order to cope—cribbing, weaving, pac-
ing—are known as vices, but they are rather the marks of a sensi-
bility forced to the brink of neurosis.

What *really* is intelligence? How would we know?

BEING SOMEONE WHO is possessed of great certainty about
what she knows, I reluctantly admit that certainty in others arous-
es deep suspicion in me. I don't know that I have ever encountered

a group of more certain-minded people than horsepeople. "Horses like that"; "oh, he doesn't mind"; "they can't do this." Really? I would ask. How do you know? And I would be met with annoyed stares for an answer. Every group of horsepeople knows better than every other, too: the Saddlebred crowd looks with disdain on the rodeo, with its bucking straps and electric prods, its broken backs and broken legs; the hunter-jumper aficionados cringe at the barbarities of the high-stepping Saddlebreds and the methods of soring the feet that often get them that way; the rodeo folk spit in the sand at the knowledge that the jumpers are being dosed with cocaine and ridden with shards of plastic in their splint boots; the practitioners of dressage assess everyone else from the lofty height of history's oldest school of equestrianism, while everyone else looks back with disbelief that forcing a horse into a frame with too-tight side reins is truly time honored, or honorable at all.

In my corner of the horse world, Dominique was certain of what she was doing; Edith was certain, too, even if sometimes they did completely different things toward the same professed end. Monica went on doing what she was doing, even if it didn't work. And I began to feel something very close to despair.

I didn't want to stop being with horses, but if the only terms on which I could do so gave me bad dreams, then I didn't know how much longer I could go on kicking the crap out of an aged pony or trotting in circles to perfect my own balance while caring nothing about what the exercise did for the one silent beneath me.

Say what you will about the Internet. For me it provided a door where I had begun to fear there was only wall. And it provided a way to journey deep into the heart of uncertainty.

IN SEARCHING THE WEB for equine welfare organizations, I came across one that recommended a book called *The Natural Horse* by Jaime Jackson, a farrier. I ordered it, and in its pages found a road map to the places I wanted to go with horses, an affirmation of my suspicions that we have been talking so loudly and continuously about what horses are like that we have blotted out the sound of their own soft snuffing protestations. Here was someone who looked at the horse with clear eyes and clear heart, and moreover someone who was willing later in brave public to turn on hundreds of years of tradition of his own profession and declare that the shoeing of horses ("No hoof, no horse," goes the equestrian world's stoutest chestnut), even "properly" done, may well be responsible for the laming and consequent disposal of uncounted horses. He, too, had invited horses to teach him, this time the mustangs of the West, and through patient observation of how social behavior affects locomotion, and how locomotion forms the hoof, he was able to posit a model for returning the horse to the state of health nature had intended. I emailed the blasphemer immediately. He wrote back, and I had found at least one person who did not find my questions annoying or extraneous. He gave me the names of several other people who also had questions instead of answers, and I began cross-country correspondences with them as well. The highest concentration of them were in the West, the locus of the recent explosion of interest in natural horsemanship, and as someone who always gravitated to the label marked "natural" over the one whose ingredients reflected faith in the promise of synthetics, I determined to go there. It did not occur to me until later that I was seeking someone whose certainties vindicated my own. And it did not occur to me till I was twenty miles beyond even that that if my certainties needed vindication, what kind of certainties were they, anyway? But there it was, the eternal lure of the guru, the one whose assurance seems so steadfast it would allow the true follower to walk on clouds, never again to fear the dreadful pestilence of questions.

I HAVE WITNESSED the following: a jumper trainer kicking a horse in the ribs with all his might for interminable minutes *(bam bam bam bam bam),* sending the echoing thumps out over the fields, while the horse stood still, uncomprehending of why; a renowned western clinician in a packed auditorium reaching the end of his young demonstration mount's ability to absorb the session's lesson but, desiring to finish making a point to his audience, banging the animal's side repeatedly until the horse froze on the verge of breakdown; a Saddlebred trainer chatting amiably while behind her a groom returned a horse to his stall and carefully fitted him with leather manacles bearing heavy silver chains; another jumper trainer becoming frustrated with the pace her new Thoroughbred was taking over the cavalletti on a longe and suddenly lashing him in the chest and neck with the longe whip until he reared back in fear.

Each one of these had followers who were grateful to sit at their feet, taking in the lesson in rapt silence. In their turn they would speak in impressive tones to their own young cadre, dispensing precious knowledge of how to make horses do the things we want them to do. I was meanwhile looking for a teacher to inform me about the teachers, to tell me the real truth. I felt certain I would know it when I heard it. Truth always has that burnished ring, does it not?

IN COLORADO I never did succeed in seeing any wild horses, even though I spent three days in a rental car attempting to navigate the pitted slot-car tracks crossing the ever fewer public lands on which they are still allowed to live their lives in service to no one but themselves. At some point I even began to enjoy the futility that obviously drenched the whole enterprise and that sent me even farther afield, talking manically into my tape recorder as I sped down long lonely roads toward another reputed wild horse area in which I felt certain I would see nothing but space. I indulged in extended verbal screeds against the hunters who were everywhere the horses should have been, since I did not know that the season had just opened and that every last person in the state was gripped with a patriotic fervor for putting bullets into warm flesh.

Returning to the lobby of my motel, I picked up a copy of a free weekly paper and read my horoscope, ever looking for guidance, even in places where it cannot be found. At one line I stopped cold, so that the elevator opened its door, then tired of waiting for me and closed again: "Sagittarius, this week the wild horses belong to you."

That was why they remained hidden from my open but unseeing eyes. What I did manage to see, the next day, was a truly remarkable demonstration of cooperative learning between horse and human in the person of Marty Marten and a black Tennessee Walker named Shadrach. The cowboy wore chaps and a Stetson and the horse wore his dressage saddle. Convention was up for grabs. Shadrach's owner wanted Marten to introduce her horse to hobbles, if only as an intellectual exercise; he was ready, she believed. And indeed, if any horse was, Shadrach was. A considered intelligence, a distinct air of gravitas, hovered about him, and the feeling you got in his presence was almost eerie, as if some being very much like a person were inside him, listening and judging you against an even higher standard of behavior than mere humans deployed. Marten talked quietly, explaining his rationales to the few people standing outside the round pen, but he did not speak to Shadrach. Instead his body said all he needed to, and for the next hour they engaged in a continuous silent dialogue. As he was bending over and attending to Shadrach's right front pastern, the horse peered over his back to see what was going on, whereupon Marten, without turning, quickly grabbed his training halter and put his head back where he wanted it. A second time, and then I saw the gears in Shadrach's brain turning: *Oh, I get it. I'm not supposed to be satisfying my own curiosity or taking a gander or nicking a little snooze; when I'm wearing my gear and I'm being handled, I'm supposed to stand at attention. Okay.*

Which was precisely what Marten explained: A horse does not know that the lesson begins at three-thirty, when you mount up, and that the forty-five minutes of grooming and handling that preceded it were not part of the deal. Indeed, Marten emphasized, everything that happens on the ground from the moment you get near your horse is the lesson that will be carried forth into the ride. All the really important stuff happens before it. Moreover, it is profoundly unfair to expect a horse who is making all the decisions when the human is on the ground to know somehow that all the rules change just because a foot is in the stirrup.

Over the course of the hour Marten worked patiently, allowing Shadrach to come up against the pressure of the rope on his feet and to discover for himself how to release it. Those gears were now turning ever faster in his brain (you could see it somehow, just as you can see it in a child who puzzles something this way and that; finally triumph flames unmistakably in the eyes as whatever falls perfectly into place). However long it took was how long it took, you could tell was Marten's approach. On top of that he added dogged consistency. It seemed unremarkably simple. But together they were nothing less than the expression of a fully formed philosophy of how to relate respectfully to any being who did not share one's language, including children, foreigners, and representatives of other species. Sitting there under the strong October sun, I felt like laughing, out of joy.

When Shadrach was reaching the end of his ability to absorb things for the day, Marten knew it and ended the session. Shadrach's owner came over to sit next to me and say, a knowing smile playing over her lips, "So, is your mind changed?"

THE MESA COUNTY FAIRGROUNDS was a festival of emptiness and dust. I drove in and parked my car under one of the three trees in this part of western Colorado and went looking for what exactly I did not know.

I had heard some éminence grise of a trainer might be there, might have some students there. At first what I found were two teenage girls eating fried chicken out of Styrofoam containers, sitting in the dust with a dog taking a nap by their sides. When I told them I was looking to learn about different ways of training horses, they both erupted at once. Well, if you want to learn anything about horses, you got to learn it from Roy Yates. All those others, forget about them. They're either phonies or fakes, and they don't know how to ride anyway. Roy says they're *afraid* to ride; notice how none of them ever gets on a horse, they just break it to saddle and that's the end of the show? Roy's a real rider, and his program takes you all the way. That's why we're here, that's why we'd follow him anywhere. We spend months here, eight hours a day, and we'll keep coming back.

Just then a pickup pulled up, and the girls were dusting off their rears as a large silver belt buckle attached to a lean white-haired man exited the truck. All of a sudden he was surrounded by laughing students who had appeared from who knew where; I had thought the long stall sheds were empty, but now I saw one of them was half-filled with horses. It was as if this man had the power to make beings appear.

I introduced myself and asked if I could observe for the afternoon. Sure, as long as you don't write all my stuff down in a book just like this other woman did, made money off what I told her when I ought to be writing my own book.

As we walked he asked me what I knew about riding, and I told him just what my dressage instructor had taught me. Well, did she always ride with spurs and two whips? he asked with an eyebrow leading the way. Did she ever tell you why there were so many "evergreens" in dressage, folks who after years of training still couldn't canter much less piaffe or passage? He mimicked in a prissy voice a lady rider testifying to her pride that she had finally learned to trot, then he snorted. You watch this, he said, and told a few of his students to get their horses ready for the afternoon mounted work.

I sat on the bleachers and watched Roy perform haunches in and out, shoulder in and out, and the slowest canter pirouette I'd ever seen, every so often pausing his horse to tell a student what to work on next. His assistant, a young woman perhaps in her mid-twenties, rode with utterly invisible aids, reins all but slack, and her horse was as light and collected and poised as petals floating on water. The last remnants of my ancient and ignorant snobbishness about western riding not really being riding were dissolved then and there; Dominique's horse looked like a perpetually drowning swimmer in comparison to this. Meanwhile other students crowded around me and kept up a chorus of "Roy says this" and "Roy says that."

In the barn I was introduced to a three-year-old Hungarian

warmblood who had recently sent two people to the hospital, including a Grand Prix dressage rider who received a broken hip. The horse was deemed fit for nothing but the glue factory, but fate had temporarily intervened to send him here. The first thing he did was to unseat Rick, the leading-man–quality trainer who was here living in a nearby motel in order that he and his wife could continue their education under Roy Yates. So they had to get "pretty rough" with the horse, including laying him down—tying together three legs and pushing him gently over onto the ground ("Not like they did it in that movie, though"). I was told this functions as a drug to the horse, who after the third or fourth time in the dirt will arise with pure peace in his eyes. Roy advocates laying every horse down, I was informed, so they learn not to become hysterical if they should fall, thrashing in barbed wire or leaping up quickly with a rider's feet still embroiled in the tack. Now the turquoise-eyed girl from Canada, who intends to become a three-day-eventer, was thinking of buying the warmblood for herself.

That night in my motel room, eating popcorn from the lobby for dinner since I arrived in the mountain town after all the restaurants had closed, the din of Yates's vociferous disciples began to fade from my ears, and I was left with a silent movie of images: the fanatic demeanor of his students; the all-too-knowing smile he wore as he took to task every other trainer currently alive; the seemingly inexplicable work with a filly, wearing a bosal, in the round pen, periodically suddenly stopped in her forward progress by a series of quick tugs on the noseband that made her back several steps with her head in the air and the whites of her eyes making crescent moons. Most of all the certainty, the absolute certainty that hung like weather over that corner of the fairgrounds.

The farther I go, I thought, wiping salt and grease from my hands with a washcloth, the farther I get from certainty. There were two possibilities, and I haven't figured out yet which was true. Either confusion is the highest form of answer, and those folks sitting at the feet of Roy Yates and his brethren, thinking they've attained enlightenment, have merely stopped thinking. Or else he is the godhead. And I am too confused to know.

25

CIRCLE RIGHT

I T ONLY LOOKS LIKE a handsomely simple black cast-iron figure of a horse, possibly Man o'War, on my mantel-piece. But it is really an occult talisman in service of an ancient hope. It is on loan from my friend and neighbor, to whom it was given as a promise that she would one day have the horses she so longed for; it worked as one wishes every promise would. If it will work for me, too, the pining that has been the highest peak on my horizon would suddenly one day disappear into level land, the moment the trailer turns in to the drive. In its place would be the horses (never one alone; how could you stand the sad sight of a herd animal all alone?) upon whom I could spy from my window as they went about their personal business. I imagine them clambering up after me through the deep shadows of the steep and rocky woodlot, a small shared adventure on our way to the upper pasture, where they would probably not notice the magnificent spread of the shimmering view down the valley that splits the mountains. But I would be happy to know they were there, on what feels like the crown of the whole green world.

Perhaps I would decide never to ride them, in deference to the long-forgotten fact that they were not made to be ridden, any more than I was made, say, to stand interminably on one leg simply because my body makes it possible. Or perhaps I would sit and watch them for days at a time, with a notebook and provisions for staying nights in a mountain pasture as I observe their movements and discussions and how much of the time they spend standing as if frozen, listening to the rustle of coyotes or deer or wild turkeys brushing past the brush. Just because I wanted to, I would take long minutes to sit close to their grazing heads, lost inside the timeless percussive music they make with the grass and ground and teeth for instruments, a bass echo responding from the density of the earth as they tear the grass from its surface, large yet impossibly subtle prehensile lips decisively sorting good herbs from bad.

Then again, I might decide to take them for a lark to a small local show where I would perform my first dressage test, no doubt very badly, but where I would become infected with the notion that with a little more application, a little more challenging, we might find ourselves with a growing taste for the addictive pleasures of work. We would start to learn what it feels like to move as one, then to merge and so to spring upward from the earth with all the strength and grace of a fictional animal.

On the day of their arrival, the longing that now pulls me through my dreams faster than I want to go, making my feet twitch against the bedsheets as I attempt to follow the silhouettes of flying tails and syncopated legs already receding toward a horizon I can never reach, will at last be gone.

WHEN I WAS a very young child, my towering sense of self-pity, coupled with the belief that my pains never got their fair due, caused me to construct a long-windedly alluring fantasy in which scientists one day would discover, to their utter and well-publicized amazement, that my nerves were fully twice as sensitive as any other human's, thus leading me to withstand hurts that would have brought anyone else to their knees. *Then* I would be both praised for my bravery and soothed for my suffering.

The very idea of connecting my name with the concept of bravery strikes me now as emblematic not so much of a six-year-old's normal hubris but a miscalculation so severe it misses the entire point, that of who I am. And that is a coward, an unfixable one. The knowledge of all the misery being endured this very moment is a torment to me, as it always has been, no matter how much I try to root it out with silent lecturing, self-flagellation, programs of desensitization, or the occasional double bourbon. I can feel insanity's hot breath against my cheek if I pause even for a moment, at which my mind always flies back to lurid full-color pictures capturing the myriad sufferings of the uncomprehending at the hands of the unmindful. Others found it amusing when a character in a movie of a decade ago spent session after session with her therapist obsessing about the garbage that was forced to wander the oceans on great barges never to find a home, but I felt a deep flash of recognition. How, indeed, to sleep when things go on and on and on?

I say it always has been thus, but there is a possibility it is getting worse. I saw exactly how far I had come when I sat down recently, in middle age, to watch a children's video of *Black Beauty*. I got to the part where Black and his doomed companion, Ginger, had been sent to the tony estate of the woman who upbraids her driver for not setting the bearing rein ever tighter, so to force the horses' heads to a suitable height. Then it was I who could bear it no longer, to stay on this hurtling narrative freight train, full steam ahead into agony with no chance of getting my hand on the brake. Anna Sewell's story could not have the effect it does—on me, on all my millions of childish compatriots—but for one literary device: the first person. And it is hearing the voiceless suddenly speak that makes me sweat and tremble, panic rising, until to save myself (because I can do nothing to save them) I must switch it off.

Freud described yours truly with unusual precision when he described children, who "have no scruples over allowing animals to rank as their full equals. Uninhibited as they are in the avowal of their bodily needs, they no doubt feel themselves more akin to animals than to their elders, who may well be a puzzle to them." My elders are nothing less than the society in which I live, even if it is composed of my peers, and they are every bit as distant from me as the adults were when I was four. Watch me read *Animal Farm,* and watch me helpless (me with my master's degree in literature from a fine university) to read it as a parable or a fairy story, as Orwell himself termed it, and not as a rousing manifesto—okay, at least the beginning. I stand up, heart full, with the animals to sing "Beasts of England"; I thrill to the speeches in which they denounce man for his wanton theft of their lives. And when the plow horse Boxer—whose repeated "I will work harder" in the face of his exploitation by cynical cheaters breaks my heart—is martyred, deceived unto the last, watch me actually cry. There. Is there any place for the likes of me?

Perhaps one, if I am willing to venture into the territory colonized by the newspapers' human-interest pages, places so curious they can only be considered entertaining interludes in reality. This exclamation mark of a place is halfway across the world, in the Rajasthan desert of western India, and is the home of the Bishnoi, a people to whom the animals and trees have no less importance than anyone else. In their history are such legends as the hundreds of villagers who sacrificed themselves to save their woody friends from loggers, and the woman whose much-reprinted old photo shows her suckling an orphaned deer. The tales of their turnabout of normal affairs, in which they will hunt down and beat anyone who attempts to hunt down the animals with whom they claim to share complete trust, are eminently cheering to me. The only other time in near memory I have read something that made me as happy was when I learned that, in the process of making a recent blockbuster movie in which some horses co-starred, the makeup used to feign equine injury was first tested with care on human skin.

Thus am I connected forever to the child I was; the moment in which I first felt love has been preserved intact inside the pain of learning that it also presumes some loss. Or else it could not matter so much you would give anything, anything, to it. The creature I have become is contained in the creature I was, and a double strand of longing has been braided into one. For the horse is nothing if not the very emblem of desire, the promise of satiety to the perpetually famished. He stands at the crest of our dreams, proud and noble, since we have no other words by which to call it. And he stands close when we wake, right at the ends of our fingers and their hunger for just this sensation, no other.

Anyway, he stands. Always Other, always somehow resolutely irreducible; there and not there. He thus embodies an essential mystery, and who doesn't love a mystery? I have certainly left you with one. I never quite nailed it: the call of Eros, child substitute, tool for power, life companion (barn talk, universal type: "Yeah, she got a fat lip kissing him Merry Christmas—he bashed her one"); all of these yet none. In attempting to explain this weird deep love for a large equid I have been like a child at the beach, digging too near the water line for the hole to do anything but fill up again with each shovelful of sand I remove.

But you know that the truest, most seductive mysteries are those that are never solved, never completely laid to rest. They remain forever alive, animated by the frictive energy of the paradoxes they enclose. And by the great, impossible dreams they realize. For the human allied with the horse is the lion lying down with the lamb, earth's most savage predator grown gentle in the presence of herbivorous prey grown unafraid. The woman with the horse is the completion of the girl with the desire for the horse, full circle into the past by embracing the present.

The picture is titled *Hope*—sentimental, to be sure, but precise. In it the big bay horse turns around to look at the person whose hand rests on his back. Their eyes have met and hold. It is unfinished. A bit vague and inscrutable. But I would hazard a guess about the artist's intention. It is about both past and future, what has been and what could be. And about the closing of distance. It seems to say: The horse will speak for us, through being voiceless. In turn, we must utter prayers for him.

A man of kindness, to his beast is kind,
But brutal actions show a brutal mind:
Remember, he, who made thee, made the brute,
Who gave thee speech and reason, formed him mute;
He can't complain, but God's omniscient eye
Beholds thy cruelty—he hears his cry!
He was designed thy servant, not thy drudge,
But know—that his Creator is thy judge.

—AUTHOR UNKNOWN (BLOOMFIELD[?]),
from *The Ladies' Equestrian Guide*, 1857

ACKNOWLEDGMENTS

THE BOOK MAY BE SHORT, but the help I received during the years I worked on it was long. Many people gave generously of their time, their stories, their suggestions, their enthusiasm. Thank you to Susan Kessler, Laura Yorke, Mary Johnson, Joan Bishop, Susan Wagner of Equine Advocates, Robin Duxbury of Project Equus, Marion Kasselle, Melanie Southard, Peter Dervis, Gypsy da Silva, Bridget de Sosio, Peggy Jett Pittenger, Janet Biggs, Wendy Klemperer, Linda Yablonsky, Patty Cronin, Annie Ellicott, Diana Coe, Peggy Whitfield, Stacie Lorenson, Judy Spillman, Jeanne Rejaunier, Virginia Ebey, Michelle Draghetti, Cheryl Hibbard, Christine Cole, Lynn Auld, Kerri Glynn, Deanne Prusak, Donna Fay Matern, Vourneen Pettigrew, Sarah Moore, Hillary Davis, Sally Rowley-Williams, Sara Smyth, Catherine Klein, Katherine Russell, Pamela Lavin, Debbie Hanzlik, Jeanette Lundgren, Mary Trager, Cynthia Reed, Mary Cochran, and Jean Craig Smith. I'm especially grateful to the extended family of Vassar College, some of whom are named here and some of whom are not (due only to faulty record-keeping). David Frost, volunteer researcher, deserves a blue ribbon. My sincere thanks go to Rina Deych.

Randlett Walster has taught me much—not only about horses but about fortitude, grace, and love.

Linda Krause continues to give me, with compassion and understanding, what I need to keep going.

Amy Cherry of Norton has once again been the editor all writers hope for but so rarely get.

And Luc Sante is, as always, the first, the last, the all.

Finally, to the horses themselves—those who have changed human history, those who have altered personal destiny, those I have ridden and known—this book is dedicated.

A NOTE ON READINGS

I HAVE DESCRIBED some of what we do to the animals we consider to be in our care; the complex psychology of how we are able to do so is explained in the works of the Swiss psychoanalyst (although she has since renounced her profession) Alice Miller, particularly *The Drama of the Gifted Child, Banished Knowledge,* and *For Your Own Good.*

Jaime Jackson's *The Natural Horse: Foundations for Natural Horsemanship* presents the theoretical and philosophical basis for treating the horse with the respect he deserves; the newsletter *The Hoof Care Advisor* puts much of it into practice by promulgating an exciting new trend that is actually old: returning the horse's hoof to its natural barefoot state and thereby obviating or curing many of the ailments now considered incurable (Star Ridge Publishing, P.O. Box 2181, Harrison, AR 72601; 1 800 409 5606).

Problem Solving is Marty Marten's eminently sensible and kind book, presenting a sound basis in groundwork with horses.

The monthly publication I would not want to do without is *The Trail Less Traveled,* a polymath guide for the student of horsemanship who is a foe of received wisdom (Winsor Publishing, 720 Front Street, Louisville, CO 80027-1805; www.ttlt.com).

Information about Premarin is available from many sources, including the Physicians Committee for Responsible Medicine (5100 Wisconsin Avenue, N.W., Suite 404, Washington, D.C.

20016; www.pcrm.org); People for the Ethical Treatment of Animals (501 Front Street, Norfolk, VA 23510; www.peta.com); and Equine Advocates (P.O. Box 670217, Flushing, NY 11367–0217; www.equineadvocates.com). The fascinating politics and economics surrounding hormone replacement therapy is detailed in *The Menopause Industry: How the Medical Establishment Exploits Women* by Sandra Coney. To learn more about alternatives to Premarin, read *Eat Right, Live Longer* by Neal Barnard, M.D., and *Menopause Without Medicine* by Linda Ojeda, Ph.D.

"What horse could even dream of a city let alone inhabit one?" This is but one of the trenchantly unanswerable questions uttered by the equine protagonist of John Hawkes's *Sweet William: A Memoir of Old Horse,* a sort of modern–day *Black Beauty.* It is well worth reading, but be warned: it takes heart.